Billy Yank & Johnny Reb

Susan Provost Beller

Billy Yank & Johnny Reb

Soldiering *in the* Civil War

Twenty-First Century Books
Brookfield, Connecticut

This book is dedicated to those who keep
Billy Yank and Johnny Reb alive—
the researchers, writers, and
reenactors of the Civil War

Photographs courtesy of Down East Books: pp. 3 (left), 20; The Library of Virginia: pp. 3 (right), 21, 78; The National Park Service, Gettysburg National Military Park: p. 8; Library of Congress: pp. 10, 17, 18, 29, 34, 41, 42, 44, 51, 75, 82 (both); Ursuline Convent Archives, Laredo, Texas: p. 11; © Corbis: p. 12; © Robert Burke 1999: p. 14; Minnesota Historical Society: p. 19; National Archives: pp. 23, 37; Chicago Historical Society: pp. 25 (ICHi-21407), 71 (ICHi-30836); Massachusetts Commandery Military Order of the Loyal Legion and the U. S. Army Military History Institute: pp. 28, 54-55, 65, 69, 76; Vermont Historical Society: pp. 33, 39; © National Geographic Society Image Collection: pp. 46 (Stephen St. John), 52 (Thad Samuels Abell II), 80 (Richard Nowitz), 81 (Richard Cooke); Congressional Medal of Honor Society: p. 49; The Western Reserve Historical Society, Cleveland, Ohio: p. 56; The Fort Delaware Society: pp. 59, 62; Andersonville National Historical Site: p. 61; Virginia Military Institute Archives: p. 66; Appomattox Court House NHP: p. 72; RG-25 Records of Special Commissions, Pennsylvania State Archives: p. 79

Published by Twenty-First Century Books
A Division of The Millbrook Press
2 Old New Milford Road
Brookfield, Connecticut 06804
www.millbrookpress.com

Copyright © 2000 by Susan Provost Beller
All rights reserved
Printed in Hong Kong
5 4 3 2 1

Library of Congress Cataloging-in-Publication Data
Beller, Susan Provost, 1949–
Billy Yank and Johnny Reb: soldiering in the Civil War/Susan
Provost Beller.
p. cm.
Includes bibliographical references (p.,) and index.
Summary: Describes military life for the average soldier in the Civil
War, including camp life, diseases, and conditions for the wounded
and prisoners of war. Includes excerpts from first-person accounts,
letters, and diaries.
ISBN 0–7613–1869–0 (lib. bdg.)
1. United States. Army—History—Civil War, 1861–1865—Juvenile
literature.   2. Confederate States of America. Army—History—
Juvenile literature.   3. United States. Army—Military life—
History—19th century—Juvenile literature.   4. Confederate
States of America. Army—Military life—Juvenile literature.
5. Soldiers—United States—History—19th century—Juvenile
literature.   6. Soldiers—Confederate States of America—
Juvenile literature.   7. United States—History—Civil War,
1861–1865—Personal narratives—Juvenile literature. [1. United
States. Army—History—Civil War, 1861–1865. 2. Confederate
States of America. Army—History. 3. United States—History—
Civil War, 1861–1865.] I. Title.

E607.B44 2000
973.7'42—dc21   99-462169

Contents

Prologue

It would be a war of many names. It would be called the War Between the States, the War of Northern Aggression, the Second War for Independence, Mr. Lincoln's War, the War of the Rebellion, and The Lost Cause. Whatever it was called, the names still used today reflect whether one lives in the North or the South.

Historians still debate the reasons for the Civil War. But no matter what triggered the war—a difference between the North and South on issues of slavery, economics, states' rights, a way of life, for example—it was a war that probably was destined to happen.

But this book is not an analysis of the reasons for the war that divided this nation. It is the story of the real-life world of Billy Yank and Johnny Reb, told in their own words. Billy Yank, as the Union soldier was commonly referred to, and Johnny Reb, the nickname given to Confederate soldiers, experienced in the Civil War what would be for most of them the most memorable event of their entire life. Their memoirs tell not just the exciting moments of battles but also the boredom of camp, the tedium of drill, and the daily battles against the more common enemies of bad food, bad camp conditions, and disease.

"There is so much suffering here that it is good to know that there are some dear ones at home safe and free from pain. We have had some fearful fighting have lost a great many men in killed wounded and missing. . . . May you never see the sights I have seen for the last week."[1] These words sent home by George Barton to his mother and sister during the horrible campaign known as the Wilderness are some of the most moving written by a Union soldier dur-

DIARIES PROVIDE A PICTURE OF SOLDIERS' DAY-TO-DAY LIVES DURING THE CIVIL WAR.

ing the Civil War. The words of the Union soldiers and their Confederate counterparts, recorded at the time in their letters or in diaries that they kept while soldiering, capture the real horrors of what it was like to be a soldier on either side during the war.

Of course, not all of the letters, diaries, and reminiscences are available. Some have been lost, some are still hidden away in someone's attic, and some were never written because the soldiers themselves did not know how to read and write. Many of the stories that would be interesting to know, like those of the black soldiers who served in the "Colored" regiments, are ones that are lost in the past. But the story of Sergeant Carney saving the flag of the 54th Massachusetts during the battle for Fort Wagner shows us that even though we may not have the same number of stories to represent some groups of soldiers, the stories were still an important part of the armies that fought for the Union and the Confederacy during the Civil War. In all, only a very small percentage of the soldiers have left us their memories. We can only wonder at all the great accounts we will never get to read.

We will hear from a number of Billy Yanks and Johnny Rebs, but the focus will be on Billy Yank Theodore Gerrish, a Union soldier from the 20th Maine Regiment, and Johnny Reb Carlton McCarthy of the Richmond Howitzers. Here are their stories.

Chapter 1
Signing Up

"The Confederate soldier," wrote Johnny Reb Carlton McCarthy, "was a venerable old man, a youth, a child, a preacher, a farmer, merchant, student, statesman, orator, father, brother, husband, son—the wonder of the world, the terror of his foes!"[1] The same might be said of his Union counterpart, Billy Yank. This fight between North and South—Union and Confederacy—pitted against each other men who had much in common and were eager to be part of the adventure of a lifetime.

War was here, and at the beginning at least, there was great enthusiasm for signing up. It would be a war of the young. About 2,700,000 soldiers would fight for the Union, while another one million fought for the Confederacy. The numbers vary among historians, but most would agree that of the 2,700,000 Union soldiers, more than two million were under twenty-one and about a million were eighteen or younger. Even these numbers were only the official ones. This was the war where younger soldiers, desperate not to miss out on their chance to fight, often enlisted under age. A piece of paper with a number 18 written on it and placed in his shoe allowed a youth to swear under oath that he was "over 18" without violating his conscience. One soldier, Joseph Bushong, claimed to have been in the army for three full years before he turned eighteen. He said that the lie he gave about his age was "the only lie I ever told in my life."[2]

Not only were they young but they were also often immigrants or sons of immigrants willing (mostly for the Union) to preserve the country that had given them a new home. There were a large

10 THIS PHOTO OF A ZOUAVE INFANTRY REGIMENT, COMPANY F OF THE 114TH PENNSYLVANIA, WAS TAKEN AT PETERSBURG, VIRGINIA, IN AUGUST 1864.

number of German regiments from their settlements in New York, Ohio, Missouri, Pennsylvania, Wisconsin, and Illinois. The Irish also provided great numbers of soldiers, perhaps the most famous being those who made up the Irish Brigade. But there were also regiments of Frenchmen, Spaniards, Italians, Scots, Swedes, Norwegians, Swiss, Welsh, Dutch, and Mexicans that fought for the Union. Many more immigrants had settled in the North than in the South, but the Confederacy was also represented by

its immigrant population; Irish and French were the two largest groups to enlist, but there were also many soldiers of Italian, German, Polish, Spanish, or Mexican background.

The soldiers on both sides were mostly farmers (about half the total), laborers, or carpenters, but it seems that all occupations were represented in at least small numbers. There were shoemakers, surveyors, blacksmiths, wheelwrights, stonecutters, butchers, masons, mechanics, merchants, printers, even teachers,

MANY CONFEDERATE TROOPS WERE OF MEXICAN OR SPANISH HERITAGE, SUCH AS THESE OFFICERS OF THE 3RD TEXAS CAVALRY. THEY ARE (L. TO R.) REFUGIO BENAVIDES, ATANACIO VIDAURRI, CRISTOBEL BENAVIDES, AND JOHN Z. LEYENDECKER.

doctors, and lawyers—any occupation of the time you could think of was probably represented in the army.

The soldiers came from all of the states, and soldiers from the North fought for the Confederacy just as soldiers from the South fought for the Union. Tiny Vermont provided the greatest number of soldiers per capita (as based on population) to the Union.

Black soldiers also fought for both the Union and the Confederacy, but their roles as Billy Yanks and Johnny Rebs were somewhat different from those of the other soldiers fighting in the Civil War. From the very beginning, black orator Frederick Douglass encouraged Abraham Lincoln to enlist black soldiers: "The arm of the slave [is] the best defense against the arm of the slaveholder."[3] But it was not until 1863, after the issuing of the Emancipation Proclamation by Abraham Lincoln, that organized black units appeared in the field for the Union. Initially they were not well received by the white officers and soldiers. They were often assigned only menial tasks. They were paid only $10 per month instead of the $13 per month salary of the white Billy Yank, and they were not allowed a clothing allowance for their uniforms. Over time they earned the respect of the

COMPANY E,
4TH U.S.
COLORED
INFANTRY,
IS SHOWN
HERE AT
FORT
LINCOLN.

white soldiers for their bravery in battle, especially for their actions at Forts Wagner, Pillow, and Hudson. About 180,000 blacks served in the Union army in 166 black regiments, and about two thirds of them were Southern blacks who had escaped from the South. But throughout the war mostly they remained under the command of white officers. A small number (about 100) of black soldiers eventually became officers, but none ever ranked higher than captain.

The Confederate army used blacks from the very beginning but not as soldiers. Initially these were just slaves brought in as laborers to take care of the camps. There are reported cases where they were made to work at gunpoint and were even put in danger by being exposed to gunfire from Union troops. Some white officers from the South, such as General Patrick R. Cleburne, argued to have the blacks serve as regular soldiers, even suggesting that those who served this way should earn their freedom by doing so. But most Southerners would have agreed with Confederate General Howell Cobb that "The day you make a soldier of them is the beginning of the end of the revolution . . .if slaves seem good soldiers, then our whole theory of slavery is wrong."[4] It wasn't until near the very end of the war in 1865 that Jefferson Davis finally ordered the recruitment of black soldiers to serve in the army.

There was one exception to this policy in the South. Early in the war in Louisiana, a group of "free persons of color" formed a regiment called the Native Guards in March 1862. When Union troops captured the city, the Native Guards remained and offered their services to the Union.

The Native Americans who fought as Billy Yanks and Johnny Rebs during the Civil War also deserve mention. At the battle of Pea Ridge in Arkansas in 1862, Native Americans fought against each other. The Confederate government actively recruited the service of the Native Americans, and Degadoga, a Cherokee known to history as Stand Watie, organized a regiment to serve the South. By the end of the war

he was a general, the highest-ranking Native American in either army. On June 23, 1865, he finally surrendered his forces to the Union. His was "the last surrender of a fighting force by a general of the Confederate armies," according to one historian.[5] About 3,500 Native Americans fought for the Union; one, Lt. Colonel Ely Parker, a Seneca, served on General Grant's personal staff from the Vicksburg Campaign in 1863 until the end of the war.

And it should be noted that even though the soldiers were nicknamed Billy Yanks and Johnny Rebs, there were also more than a few Betty Yanks and Jane Rebs. Mary Livermore, who recorded the work of the Sanitary Commission after the war, estimated that there were about 400 women who dressed and fought as men for the Union cause during the Civil War. Some were wives who snuck into the army to be with their husbands. Others were just girls and women who were determined to be part of this great adventure. Many were discovered and sent home, but some actually fought throughout the entire war.

The stories of these female soldiers are not as widely known as those of their brother Billy Yanks

14 and Johnny Rebs. But any story about the Civil War soldiers has to at least acknowledge their presence in both armies and their role in the war. Long before the women's suffrage movement, there were women showing their patriotism by dying for their country. Union General William Hays sent in a report on the burial of dead soldiers after the Battle of Gettysburg in July 1863. His troops buried 1,629 bodies—387 Union soldiers and 1,242 Confederates. He noted that one of the Confederate bodies was "One female (private), in rebel uniform."[6] Not all the women served as privates, either. At least one served as a Confederate lieutenant and another as a major in the Union army.

Rosetta Wakeman, who served as Private Lyons Wakeman with the 153rd New York Volunteers, wrote home that she was "enjoying myself first rate." She wrote regularly, signing her letters with her real name and assuring everyone that she loved the work of soldiering and was not afraid to die: "If it is God['s] will for me to be killed here, it is my will to

DURING THE CIVIL WAR, ROSETTA WAKEMAN DISGUISED HERSELF AND SERVED AS A MAN, PRIVATE LYONS WAKEMAN.

die." As a prison guard, she wrote that she knew of a woman who was being held in prison for breaking the "regulation of war" by leading her troops into battle. Rosetta Wakeman excitedly wrote: "When the Rebels bullets was acoming like a hail storm she rode her horse and gave orders to the men."[7] Rosetta Wakeman did not survive the war, dying of dysentery after a long hospital stay in 1864. No mention was made that she was a woman, and historians guess that perhaps she held on to her secret to the very end. She was buried as Lyons Wakeman in New Orleans, where she had died.

The Civil War was great adventure for all the soldiers. One of the most striking features in the letters, diaries, and reminiscences that remain from the soldiers was their awareness that this was the most exciting time of their lives. Rosetta Wakeman was not the only one enjoying herself. Billy Yank Theodore Gerrish wrote: "Everything was new and exciting to my boyish vision."[8] His Confederate counterpart, Johnny Reb Carlton McCarthy, looking back after the war on the defeat of the rebel army, could still write that for all of them, "the deadly struggle marked a grand period in their history!"[9]

Chapter 2
Becoming a Soldier

"The first thing in the morning is drill, then drill, then drill again. Then drill, drill, a little more drill. Then drill, and lastly drill. Between drills, we drill and sometimes stop to eat a little and have a roll-call."[1] Oliver W. Norton of the 83rd Pennsylvania Regiment captured perfectly Billy Yank and Johnny Reb's feelings about drill. It was the most complained-about part of the soldier's day, and along with the food, it was the part of the soldier's life that they most often wrote home about. The soldiers, both Union and Confederate, could not understand the purpose of all this drill.

They had enlisted and left home eager to fight. But instead of meeting the enemy in battle and defeating him, all they did was drill—company drill, regimental drill, brigade drill, division drill. They recognized that some drill was necessary. Theodore Gerrish of the 20th Maine Regiment wrote of his regiment's pathetic attempt at order as they marched into Washington in September 1862 to join the war: "It was a most ludicrous march. We had never been drilled, and we felt that our reputation was at stake. An untrained drum corps furnished us with music; each musician kept different time, and each man in the regiment took a different step. Old soldiers sneered; the people laughed and cheered; we marched, ran, walked, galloped, and stood still, in our vain endeavor to keep step."[2]

Theirs was not the only regiment to need drill in order to march like soldiers as they began the war. But from the soldiers' point of view, they were drilled much too often. The officers thought otherwise. And the experience of both the Northern and Southern armies in the first major battle at Manassas, Virginia, on July 21, 1861, proved that all of the drill so far had been far from enough.

SOLDIERS OFTEN WROTE HOME ABOUT THE SEEMINGLY ENDLESS DRILLS THEY HAD TO UNDERGO.

Abraham Lincoln had encouraged his general, Irvin McDowell, to meet the rebels in battle. The troops were mostly ninety-day troops, and their enlistment period was almost up. McDowell argued that the soldiers had not had enough training to fight a major battle, that the troops were still green. But Lincoln had responded: "You are green, it is true, but they are green also; you are green alike."[3]

No one could have predicted what actually happened when this order was obeyed. Everyone on both sides had "known" from the beginning that this was going to be a one-battle war. The armies would meet.

A battle would be fought. Northerners thought the Union would win, while Confederates, who believed that "One Southern man is equal to three Yankees," felt that their side would be victorious. Whoever won, peace would be negotiated after this single battle. So everyone wanted the chance to be present at the battle of a lifetime. Soldiers had hurried to enlist, fearing they would miss the fight. And as the battle neared, the citizens of Washington also wanted to be sure to have front-row seats for the spectacle. McDowell would have to contend not only with his green troops but also with the civilians who packed

18 their picnic baskets and headed to the countryside in their carriages following the soldiers, as if this was the greatest social event of the year.

Reluctantly McDowell moved his army to meet the Confederates, noting with disgust that "They stopped every moment to pick blackberries or get water; they would not keep in the ranks, order as much as you pleased."[4]

Manassas was a hard-fought battle. At several points in the conflict it looked as if either the Union or Confederates were about to win. In the end, the Confederates were victorious.

At Fairfax Court House at the end of the battle, McDowell would report: "The men having thrown away their haversacks in the battle and left them behind, they are without food. . . . The larger part of the men are a confused mob, entirely demoralized."[5]

Others would defend the actions of the soldiers: "There was no general demoralization in the army, although many of the troops acted like all novices in the dreadful art of war, and executed some movements with great confusion."[6]

CHILDREN WERE AMONG THE CIVILIANS WHO WATCHED THE TROOPS IN ACTION.

The Confederates defeated General Irvin McDowell and his Union troops at the first major battle at Manassas, Virginia, on July 21, 1861.

However one interpreted the actions of Billy Yank that day, leadership on both sides of the conflict saw it as a near disaster. There would have to be even more drill for Billy Yank and Johnny Reb before the armies could meet in battle again.

The soldiers of both sides would also have to accept the reality of being soldiers. They would have to learn to follow orders. The indignant words of Private Johnny Haley of the 17th Maine spoke for most of the Billy Yanks and Johnny Rebs: "How strange it seems to us who have enjoyed our freedom so recently to be thus deprived of all privileges. Have we enlisted to secure freedom for others only to give up our own?"[7]

But the realities of military life meant that they did indeed have to give up much of their personal freedom in order to become effective soldiers. Wrote Johnny Reb Carlton McCarthy, "It took years to teach the educated privates in the army that it was their duty to give unquestioning obedience to officers because they were such, who were awhile ago their playmates and associates in business."[8] Billy Yank

Theodore Gerrish observed the same about his fellow soldiers: "One of the most difficult things in the world for a genuine Yankee to do, was to settle down, and become accustomed to the experience of a soldier's life. He was naturally inquisitive, and wanted to know all the reasons why an order was given, before he could obey it."[9]

Not only privates had that difficulty. One of the problems at Manassas had been the unwillingness of the officers of regiments on both sides to accept orders from their own higher-ranking officers. Each seemed willing to conduct war as he alone saw fit. Billy Yanks like Theodore Gerrish could comment bitterly on the "couple of gilt straps upon the shoulders of one who at home was far beneath him" that now made him into an officer.[10] The officers themselves were also too conscious of the rank those markings on their shoulders gave them and were reluctant to take orders from anyone.

The drill of the future would not be just for the soldiers of individual regiments, but for regiments

BILLY YANK JOHN HALEY OF THE 17TH MAINE, PHOTOGRAPHED IN JANUARY 1863

JOHNNY REB CARLTON McCARTHY OF
THE RICHMOND HOWITZERS

and brigades and divisions until the whole army, officers and men, had learned to move as one. With the first major battle of the Civil War over, Billy Yank and Johnny Reb would now learn to become soldiers. Johnny Reb Carlton McCarthy's comment on the Confederate soldier really fit both sides: "The Confederate soldier was peculiar in that he was ever ready to fight, but never ready to submit to the routine duty and discipline of the camp or on the march."[11] Billy Yank Theodore Gerrish also described both when he wrote of the Union soldier: "Accustomed to be independent, the words *go* and *come* grated harshly upon his ear."[12]

Before the two armies met again in battle, Billy Yank and Johnny Reb would have countless drills to prepare them to do a much better job than either side had done at Manassas. By the time the war was in its second year, discipline would become a way of life for them and they would have heard *go* and *come* enough times that it would become second nature for them to obey their orders.

Chapter 3
Life in Camp

Another fancy idea was that the principal occupation of a soldier should be actual conflict with the enemy. They did n't [*sic*] dream of such a thing as camping for six months at a time without firing a gun, or marching and countermarching to mislead the enemy, or driving wagons and ambulances, building bridges, currying horses, and the thousand commonplace duties of the soldier."[1] Johnny Reb Carlton McCarthy's description is very accurate. There were actually Billy Yanks and Johnny Rebs who served through the entire Civil War and never were involved in a major battle. Even Billy Yanks and Johnny Rebs whose careers included a great deal of fighting spent the overwhelming amount of their time either in camp, on guard duty, or on the march.

When not involved in drill or guard duty, life in camp revolved around cooking and eating, improving one's housing, recreation, and letters from home. Cooking and eating were big topics and, along with complaints about drill, were the most frequently written-about items in letters home.

Billy Yank and Johnny Reb spent a lot of their free time improving their living arrangements. Especially as winter neared and the soldiers knew that they most likely would not be fighting until the spring, the effort to create comfortable winter quarters became a major focus of their lives. Union soldier Thomas Owen from New York wrote home in January 1863: "We are now in a fine place. It is in a pine woods. We have built up our tents with logs so that they are very nice and warm. . . . Think some of moving soon, which don't please us much now that we have such a nice place." The next winter he was bragging "We are fixing up good winter quarters." That "good winter quarters" could make a difference in Billy Yank's attitude is

TYPICAL WINTER QUARTERS
WERE SMALL LOG HUTS
CONSTRUCTED AROUND
REGULAR-ISSUE TENTS.
SOLDIERS MADE WALKWAYS
OF SHORT POLES LAID
CLOSELY TOGETHER.

reflected in Owen's letter home a few months later: "Tell her not to worry about me in the least for I am well and have comfortable quarters. Very good living. In fact, I am enjoying myself."[2]

Johnny Reb McCarthy gives his own account of the soldier's attempt to create a home away from home. He talked of the soldiers' excitement as they learned they were about to go into winter quarters. "Hasty plans for comfort and convenience are eagerly discussed till late into the night, and await only the dawn of another day for execution."[3] McCarthy goes on to discuss the various styles of winter quarters developed by the soldiers and devotes several pages in his memoir to the process of settling down for the winter. There is no mistaking the enthusiasm of this Johnny Reb for setting up just the right camp.

Once settled into a camp, whether a temporary camp or more permanent winter quarters, Billy Yank and Johnny Reb turned their thoughts to recreation and the comforts they missed from home. Carlton McCarthy described being in winter quarters as "a good time to make and carve beautiful pipes of hard wood with horn mouth-pieces, very comfortable chairs, bread trays, haversacks, and a thousand other conveniences."[4]

Many of the recreational items created were for personal use. But there were even some cases where elaborate building projects were undertaken by the soldiers in winter quarters. A group of soldiers belonging to the Irish Brigade built themselves a church. Peter Welsh wrote home about the finished product: "The 88th have an enclosure mad[e] in front of the chaplins tent with ceder [cedar] bushes and that forms the church with the little alter [altar] in the tent inside."[5] A Rhode Island unit of Billy Yanks built log cabins for their officers and then a church that even included a fireplace and a chandelier made out of tin cans!

Once settled into camp, and when not drilling or eating, the soldiers amused themselves with dice games, smoking their clay pipes and, often, drinking. Drunkenness was sometimes a problem for the bored soldiers in camp, and good officers kept the men busy to keep them out of trouble. Officers also tried to arrange religious services in an attempt to keep trouble in the camps to a minimum. But considering the number of soldiers, the problems were fairly few. Johnny Reb McCarthy captured the life of the soldier in camp this way: "He played marbles, spun his top, played at foot-ball, bandy, and hop-scotch; slept quietly, rose early, had a good appetite, and was happy. He had time now comfortably to review the toils, dangers, and hardships of the past campaign."[6]

According to Billy Yank Theodore Gerrish, the soldier also had time for "the practical, good-natured jokes we used to practice upon each other."[7] He tells of distracting the cook to grab more than their share of the doughnuts he was making, and other pranks,

OFFICERS OF THE 82ND ILLINOIS IN CAMP AT ATLANTA, GEORGIA, IN 1864 GAMBLE TO PASS THE TIME.

but he seems to most enjoy the story of the picket post. Apparently, a new recruit arrived and was concerned that he would not know what to do when assigned picket duty (the soldiers assigned to guard the camp boundaries at night). Gerrish led the others as they convinced the recruit that picket duty was performed standing on top of a small pointed top post so that the soldier had a good view of the surrounding area. Then he proceeded to create a post for the recruit to practice standing on. It wasn't until an officer arrived that the poor recruit, who had been trying to balance on the post for hours, was advised of how picket duty was really performed. Gerrish counted it as one of their most successful pranks.

26 The most cherished activity for both Billy Yank and Johnny Reb revolved around writing letters home and receiving and reading their mail. Union officer Elisha Rhodes from Rhode Island captured the soldier's need for word from home very well in his diary entry for March 6, 1865: "We have received no mail for several days and do not like it. A soldier can do without hard bread but not without his letters from home."[8] Peter Welsh of the 28th Massachusetts had a similar complaint in a letter home: "i have not received any letter from you for over a month allthough i have wrote several letters to you since."[9] Billy Yank Theodore Gerrish spoke sadly and movingly of those who didn't receive any letters. Mail was important since "Each letter received was like a messenger from home, and was an additional cord binding our hearts to our loved ones."[10]

On the other hand, at times the messages from home could be painful ones. Black Union soldiers who came from border states that still had slave populations worried that their families at home might face harassment from the slaveowners in the community. Imagine the distress of the soldier receiving the following letter from home: "I have had nothing but trouble since you left. You recollect what I told you how they would do after you was gone. they abuse me because you went . . . and beat me scandalously the day before yesterday . . . You ought not to left me in the fix I am in & all these little helpless children to take care of."[11]

But for Billy Yank and Johnny Reb, the most significant benefit of a long stay in camp was that the food, that most important part of a soldier's life, was better and more plentiful than when they were on the march.

Chapter 4
Food

"Our rations were for the most part good and plenty of it . . . hard tac . . . that sometimes had to be broken with your heel or musket. Soft bread when in a permanent camp. Fresh beef. Salt junk (pork). Salt horse (beef). Peas. Beans. Potatoes. Desecated vegetables. Rice etc."[1] Alfred Bellard from New Jersey was not unhappy with the rations fed to soldiers in the Union army. However, it was much more common to hear negative comments than his fair assessment quoted above.

Johnny Reb Carlton McCarthy was less generous in his description of the Confederate rations. "Sometimes there was an abundant issue of bread, and no meat; then meat in any quantity, and no flour or meal; sugar in abundance, and no coffee to be had for 'love or money;' and then coffee in plenty, without a grain of sugar."[2]

In actual fact, supplying the soldiers with the rations that they were entitled to receive when they needed them was a nightmare for the quartermasters in both armies. When the armies were in camp, the job was done adequately enough to keep Billy Yank and Johnny Reb at least reasonably content. It is true that as the war progressed, Johnny Reb increasingly had to do with half rations and sometimes none at all. But it is important to remember that most of the war was fought on Southern soil, and Johnny Reb received a great deal of food from the citizens in the area who were more than happy to show support for the loyal sons of the South. Billy Yank, on the other hand, had the advantage of sutlers' wagons, which did a wonderful business (especially right after the soldiers received their pay!) supplying supplementary goods like cakes and pies and better food.

AN ENTERPRISING MAN SET UP THIS FRUIT AND OYSTER HOUSE TO SELL FOOD AND OTHER SPECIALTY ITEMS TO THE TROOPS.

In spite of the best efforts of the quartermasters, however, the complaints about food in the letters home are extremely common. Countless are the descriptions of hard tack that was inedible even after soaking, meat covered with maggots, and food issued to the regiment that never got past the officers' mess.

The real hardships that occurred, especially for Billy Yank, were when he was on the march. Orders were routinely given forbidding foraging in the countryside, and soldiers were often severely punished if they broke those commands. But the inability to keep the marching army supplied caused any number of complaints to be sent home. The worst cases were on the western front, where the war was waged over a much larger area and where supplying communities were quite far away. Union drummer William Bircher

AFRICAN AMERICANS OFTEN SERVED AS COOKS IN THE UNION ARMY. NUMEROUS LETTERS AND DIARIES RECORD HOW IMPORTANT FOOD WAS TO THE SOLDIERS.

from Minnesota recorded his disgust with the food situation in his diary in 1863. "We were very short of rations. We had not had a bean or any salt pork issued us for a month, and with those articles cut off from the soldiers' bill of fare life was not worth living, and patriotism and love of country must take second place."[3]

As the Civil War progressed, the story for Johnny Reb became one of near starvation. The effectiveness of the Northern blockade, along with the inflation that sent prices skyrocketing, helped to cause real scarcity and severe hunger throughout the South. The soldiers probably ate better than some of the people living in the big cities like Richmond, but they often had to supplement their food in a gruesome way. After battle, it was not uncommon for Johnny Reb to pick through the pockets and haversacks of the dead and wounded still on the field for something edible.

The food situation became so critical that by July 1863 some units were officially informed that their mules could be killed and mule meat given to the soldiers for their rations. Some food items that were supposed to be part of the Confederate soldiers' rations, like coffee, became impossible to find.

This led to a great deal of barter between Billy Yank and Johnny Reb, something that was frowned upon by the officers. When the armies were camped near each other, the exchange of goods by the soldiers became rather common. Johnny Reb had tobacco, increasingly rare in the North since it was grown in the South. Billy Yank, of course, had food, and the two sides seemed quite capable of exchanging items at night and then fighting with each other the following morning.

Billy Yank and Johnny Reb may have found much cause for grievances about their provisions, but one also has to pity the life of their quartermasters. Confederate quartermaster Silas Grisamore probably expressed the feelings of both the Union quartermasters and himself when he wrote: "No persons connected with the Confederate armies received so much abuse as the quartermasters. . . . Let forage be plenty or scarce, let the roads be good or bad, let the sun shine or the rain fall, subsistence had to be procured, provisions transported."[4]

Chapter 5
Dirt, Lice, and Disease

"Looking at the shirt I had just removed, I found it full all of—excuse the word—clothes lice, or 'greybacks'. . . . It is easy to laugh about this now, but sensitive persons fairly shudder at the thought of this pestilence, worse in nature than many of the Egyptian plagues."[1] Irish Brigade chaplain Father William Corby's encounter with "greybacks" was only one of the annoying and often even deadly facets of camp life.

As hard as it is to imagine, two out of every three deaths in the Civil War were from disease, not from battle wounds. Billy Yank and Johnny Reb faced a life not only of bad food but also of poor sanitary conditions and exposure to diseases that actually killed off more soldiers than did bullets. Billy Yank Theodore Gerrish captured the sadness of these numbers when he wrote: "There is some inspiration to die in the shock of conflict, amidst the crash of contending hosts, to pass away in a whirlwind of fire; but there is no satisfaction in struggling with disease, and to grow weak and shadowy under its touch, and to know from the beginning that death is the only relief."[2]

Reporting in 1867 on camp conditions during the war, Union Doctor Roberts Bartholow wrote about the recruits' arrival in camp. "As soon after enlistment as possible, the recruit is hurried to the depot; he is supplied with army rations badly cooked and uncleanly served; he is drilled vigorously several hours each day; at night, furnished with one or two blankets and occasionally a little straw, he is thrust into a tent with a large number of others, or into crowded temporary quarters, where he is subjected to horribly impure air, frequently to cold and dampness, and always to excessive discomfort, or he is required to perform a tour of guard duty which interrupts his habit of nightly repose; but slender opportunities of washing and bathing are afforded him, and he is at all times exposed to the influences of the unwholesome air of badly-policed camps and quarters, and to the emanations from his comrades suffering under various contagious maladies."[3]

In fact, new troops arriving at the camps around Washington for training often found their first battle to be against measles, mumps, and other diseases, as soldiers, living together in large groups for the first time, shared their germs with others around them. Only after this process of toughening up were the survivors trained to fight.

After having survived the early exposure to measles, the recruits moved on to the more common problems of camp life, those identified by Dr. Bartholow. Dysentery, what we usually call diarrhea, was an almost constant companion of the soldiers. No one knew why some regiments were healthier than others, and doctors explored all sorts of theories trying to determine how to prevent dysentery. One doctor even recommended that drinking the blood of a freshly killed animal would prevent diarrhea.

Billy Yank Theodore Gerrish gave the soldier's perspective on camp conditions: "The men were unused to the climate, the exposure, and the food, so that the whole experience was in direct contrast to their life at home." But he saved his greatest disgust for the hospitals where sick soldiers had to go for treatment: "The buildings used as hospitals were but illy adapted to such a purpose, being very imperfect in ventilation, cleanliness, and general convenience."[4] Gerrish shared the common soldier's fear of the medical treatment they would receive if they reported an illness. Like many other soldiers, he preferred to stay in the care of his friends rather than go to the regimental hospitals. In fact, looking back with the medical knowledge of today, we know that the key to health was sanitation, sometimes something as simple as making sure that the latrines did not foul the drinking water.

Black soldiers had even more cause to worry about their medical care than Gerrish did. There was a serious problem in getting doctors willing to serve with the black regiments. One historian notes that

REGIMENTAL HOSPITALS FREQUENTLY WERE LITTLE MORE THAN A FEW TENTS. THIS PHOTO IS OF THE HOSPITAL OF THE 12TH VERMONT.

"As a result, hospital stewards were appointed to the posts of assistant surgeon and surgeon in the black regiments, where they performed many duties for which they were not qualified, including surgery." Although an attempt was made to remedy the situation, he notes that "the lack of adequate medical care in the black regiments persisted to the end of the war."[5]

Personal cleanliness was another issue. Even in the regiments where sanitation was good and disease rates were lower, such as the 2nd Rhode Island Volunteers, the captain of the regiment could still write about the misery of not having had a chance to change clothes during five weeks of heavy marching and fighting. Many of the soldiers did not have addi-

34 FATHER CORBY (FAR RIGHT) WAS CHAPLAIN OF THE IRISH BRIGADE. HIS MEMOIRS GIVE A PICTURE OF SOLDERING DURING THE CIVIL WAR.

tional clothing and went months at a time without the opportunity to get clean, suffering from "long, tedious marches under a scorching sun, with dust penetrating every particle of . . . clothing, or under pelting rain and through mud knee-deep," in the words of Father Corby.[6] Letters home and diaries kept by the soldiers speak of their exhaustion from marches that denied them real rest for several days in a row. Often they would stop for the night, but without the wagons to provide food and their tents, the soldiers would sleep in the cold and mud only to face another long day of marching in the morning.

The dirt, the bad and inadequately cooked food, the days of hunger alternating with times of gorging when food became available again, the lack of personal cleanliness, the use of impure drinking water—

all these added up to conditions so horrible that one has to wonder how anyone was fit to face an enemy in battle. It is important to note that doctors were actually pleased with the disease rate of only 60 percent. In the Mexican War of 1846–1848, 88 percent of the deaths had been from disease.

Finally, to return to Father Corby's "greybacks," he claimed the Union soldiers encountered them upon moving into camps that the Confederates had just left during the Peninsula Campaign: "They had been left to us as a legacy, and were the sole inhabitants of the huts that had been evacuated by the routed enemy."[7] There is at least one Johnny Reb who disagrees with who brought the "graybacks" (his spelling) to whom: "The grayback was never here until Lincoln's soldiers came, and the easy presumption is that they brought him along with them and turned him loose on us. Did not the Yankees bring the chicken cholera, the hog cholera, women-in-breeches, and various other pests and plagues?"[8]

Chapter 6
On the March

William Bircher was only fifteen years old when he joined the 2nd Regiment, Minnesota Veteran Volunteers as their drummer boy in 1861. Bircher kept a detailed diary of his years as a Union soldier. Each day he recorded the weather and the number of miles that he marched, along with information on what happened. At the end of each year he totaled up the number of miles that he had marched. The totals are shocking. In 1862 the total number of miles that he and his colleagues had marched was 1,493; 1863 was a good year for the unit with only 917 miles of marching. But in 1864 the Minnesota soldiers would march an incredible 2,689 miles. There were many, many days when William Bircher's diary recorded marches of over 20 miles.

Both Billy Yank and Johnny Reb might complain about the boredom of life in camp, but several days on the march would have them writing home with a new set of complaints. "No pen can describe the sufferings and physical exhaustion of an army of infantry marching thirty miles a day," wrote Billy Yank Theodore Gerrish in his memoir.[1] It was the generals, of course, who decided when the army needed to be on the move. And their decisions had to be strategic ones. Obviously the leaders on both sides wished to order their armies to be on the march only when the weather was good. That way the armies could make the best time in getting to whatever place their generals needed them to be. But the weather often did not cooperate.

It is hard to tell from the accounts what would be considered good marching weather. The complaints of Billy Yank and Johnny Reb pretty much cover any kind of conditions on the march. It seemed that either the roads were too dry and the dust kicked up

THESE TROOPS OF THE 6TH
MAINE INFANTRY POSED FOR A
PHOTO BEFORE SETTING OUT ON
YET ANOTHER MARCH.

37

by the marching armies would choke them as they trudged along, or there would be torrential rains and they would have to slog through knee-deep mud. Confederate Cadet Jack Stanard, on the march with the other cadets from the Virginia Military Institute in 1864, wrote home to his mother about one of those muddy marches: "the roads were awful *perfect loblolly* all the way and we had to wade through like *hogs*."[2]

Johnny Reb Carlton McCarthy gives a vivid picture of the misery of marching on the dry roads. "The nostrils of the men, filled with dust, became dry and feverish, and even the throat did not escape. The 'grit' was felt between the teeth, and the eyes were rendered almost useless. There was dust in eyes, mouth, ears, and hair."[3] But fellow Confederate soldier John Worsham of Stonewall Jackson's Foot Cavalry—so called because they could march almost as fast as mounted soldiers—dreaded more the rainy marches. He describes the progress of the water through his clothing until he gets so wet that "the storm within him breaks loose, resulting in his cursing the Confederacy, the generals, and everything in the army, including himself!"[4]

The marches were also often long, especially if bad weather had the army running behind schedule. Billy Yank Gerrish wrote of seeing men "limp and reel and stagger as they endeavor to keep up with their regiments. These men were doubtless acquainted with fatigue before they entered the army," he noted, "but this fearful strain in marching so many miles, in heavy marching order, for successive days, is too much for them. Brave, strong men fall fainting by the wayside."[5]

At the end of the long days of marching, even if conditions were good, Billy Yank and Johnny Reb had to face the fact that often their supply trains would not keep up with the marching soldiers. When soldiers were given orders to march, they were told to pack the amount of food they would need for a cer-

tain number of days. If the march continued longer, there was no guarantee that their supplies could catch up with the soldiers. That meant that the soldiers might run out of food or have to sleep alongside the road without their tents. Father Corby describes an early march of the Irish Brigade: "In the morning we had placed everything in an army wagon . . . so that we were now left without anything to eat and with nothing to sleep on. . . . But, you may ask, where are the materials that were put into the army wagon? They are there, but the wagons are 'stuck in the mud'—Virginia mud—ten or fifteen miles behind. Next morning we rose from the ground!—to march! No breakfast, and, as we advanced, we left the army wagons still farther behind us."[6]

It also did not help that at times the lack of sleep came not just from lack of shelter but also from the fact that the soldiers continued marching well into the night. When finally told to halt, they could not even see well enough to pick out a good location for camp. Union soldier George F. Williams remembered a night when they marched until 1:00 A.M.: "Then came the welcome order to lie down and rest.

A SUPPLY TRAIN SUCH AS THIS ONE FOLLOWED SOLDIERS ON THE MARCH. MANY TIMES THE SUPPLIES DID NOT ARRIVE WHEN THE SOLDIERS CAMPED FOR THE NIGHT.

As the column halted in the darkness, the men threw themselves on the narrow strips of sward by the road-side, sleeping in long rows as they lay wrapped in their blankets and ponchos."[7]

There *was* one benefit to being on the march. The soldiers, both Billy Yank and Johnny Reb, felt that much of their time spent in camp was wasted. At least when they went out on the march, there was a feeling that they were moving. If they were moving, it meant that they were on their way to a battle. Battles had their horrors, but being in battle might mean that the end of the war was closer. So the soldiers welcomed the order to pack rations and prepare for a march. Johnny Reb Carlton McCarthy summed it up this way: "After all, the march had more pleasure than pain."[8]

Chapter 7
Words From the Front Lines

Of all the material written by soldiers on both sides, nothing compares with their accounts of the horrors of the battlefield. It is in these words, written by Billy Yank and Johnny Reb at the time of the battles, that we come to see how "seeing the elephant," as they called seeing combat for the first time, changed their lives forever. From the chaotic battle at Manassas in 1861 to the closing scenes near Petersburg in 1865, Billy Yank and Johnny Reb witnessed carnage on a scale that had never been experienced before by Americans. Their words from the front lines are all that is needed to understand what they experienced.

From Manassas, "I remember that my first sensation was one of astonishment at the peculiar whir of the bullets," wrote Elisha Rhodes of the 2nd Rhode Island Regiment.[1] Wrote a Johnny Reb from Georgia: "I didn't come out here to fight this way; I wish the earth would crack open and let me drop in."[2] But Manassas in July 1861 was not the expected "only battle of the war"—it was only the first in a long series of bloody battles that Billy Yank and Johnny Reb would have to get used to fighting. The "peculiar whir of the bullets" would become an all too familiar sound.

The following spring the war began in earnest, with soldiers who knew they were committed to serve a three-year term and who had months of training. The first major engagement was in the West, at Shiloh, in Tennessee. Hurrying forward to support a Confederate line that was beginning to weaken, Sam Watkins came upon his first sight of battle: "Men were lying in every conceivable position; the dead lying with their eyes wide open, the wounded begging piteously for help. . . . It all seemed to me a dream."[3] A Union soldier enduring that Confederate attack watched in amazement as "A rabbit, trembling with fear, rushes out of the brush in which the rebel battery is hidden and snuggles up close to a soldier, his natural terror of man entirely subdued by the dreadful surroundings."[4]

In the East meanwhile, the Union Army of the Potomac, commanded by popular General George B. McClellan, was attempting to work its way to Richmond, Virginia, the Confederate capital, by the back route, up the peninsula between the York and James Rivers. McClellan's army and the Confederate Army of Northern Virginia fought a series of battles that became known as the Peninsula Campaign. After two months on the peninsula, McClellan's army began to retreat to its starting point. This would be no rout as at Manassas, but rather a disciplined retreat under fire. It is the horror of this retreat that stayed in the minds of the participants. Wrote Union soldier George Williams: "For seven weary days we fought from early dawn until far into the night. . . . Battle after battle was fought, until we ceased count-

THIS LARGE FIELD HOWITZER WAS USED IN THE BATTLE OF SEVEN PINES, VIRGINIA, WHICH WAS PART OF THE PENINSULA CAMPAIGN, MAY–AUGUST 1862.

ing the engagements. . . . We struggled through swamps, and waded swollen streams. . . . Amidst a hellish confusion of sounds we fought on . . . fighting with the courage born of despair."[5]

42 The campaigns of 1862 continued with the Johnny Rebs earning most of the honors. The year would end with two of the most horrific battles in American history. The first was fought in September near Sharpsburg, Maryland, along Antietam Creek and earned itself the dubious honor of becoming the date on which more Americans died or were wounded in battle than on any other day in our history. The most powerful accounts of this battle describe two fights—one in a cornfield bordered by woods, the other on a small sunken farm road. The cornfield ground was bitterly contested, and the Union and Confederate armies together lost about 6,000 soldiers there in fighting that at times was hand to hand. As the armies moved back and forth, wounded soldiers who might have been saved were trampled to death or shot yet again. Wrote one Union soldier, Eugene Powell from Ohio, "The sight at the fence, where the enemy was standing when we gave our first fire, was awful beyond description . . . dead men were literally piled upon and across each other."[6]

The fight at the sunken road, which would be forever known as Bloody Lane, was another story of death. Here, after countless charges by Union troops, including the Irish Brigade's most costly fight of the war, the Confederates on the sunken road were finally defeated. But they were not able to retreat. They died on the road, and the photographs taken several days later of their bodies lying on top of each other shocked the nation.

And the year was not over. In December, the Union army would attempt to dislodge the Confederates from a fortified hill near Fredericksburg, Virginia. Father Corby would write bitterly that "the place into which Meagher's brigade [The Irish Brigade] was sent was simply a slaughter pen . . . our brigade was cut to pieces."[7]

The 1863 campaigns opened with another major Confederate victory at Chancellorsville, Virginia. This gave General Robert E. Lee the confidence to move his troops north again, this time up into Pennsylvania, to what would be the most important battle of the war, Gettysburg. After two days of fighting, what is probably the most famous attack in American history took place there. General Lee chose Lt. General James Longstreet to coordinate the attack and General George Pickett to lead the charge. When

Longstreet ordered the advance, Pickett marched the 12,000 men under his command across one mile of open fields to attack the Union troops on Cemetery Ridge. Amazingly, many of the Johnny Rebs made it to the enemy positions, and the fighting there was hand to hand. As it began to appear that Pickett's Charge might actually succeed, it was a group of Vermont regiments who helped save the Union army. Wheelock Veazey, commanding the 16th Vermont, led the charge. "With a mighty shout the rush forward was made, and, before the enemy could change his front, we had struck his flank, and swept down the line."[8] As General Pickett's Johnny Rebs retreated back across the field, the Confederacy lost its best chance to end the war on its terms.

The fighting of 1863 continued with major battles on the western front at Chickamauga in Georgia and Chattanooga in Tennessee. The East remained quiet, but all that would change with the appointment of General Grant to head the Union Army of the Potomac on March 9, 1864. Ulysses S. "Unconditional Surrender" Grant was the hero of Shiloh and Vicksburg. President Lincoln appreciated him for his

IN A TURNING POINT OF THE WAR, THE UNION FORCES DEFEATED THE CONFEDERATES AT GETTYSBURG.

determination and his philosophy of continuing to fight even when he suffered setbacks. Grant led the Army of the Potomac through a series of huge and costly battles in 1864 that ended with a siege at Richmond and Petersburg, Virginia, that would ultimately bring the war to an end in April 1865.

The campaign opened at the Wilderness in May 1864, where soldiers had to deal not only with fighting but also with finding the decomposing bodies of soldiers who had died on the same ground in the Chancellorsville battle the year before. This battle was a scene from hell as the fire of the rifles set the dry underbrush on fire, burning alive about two hundred soldiers who could not be moved to safety in time. Billy Yank Theodore Gerrish of Maine was there and remembered "a medley of sounds,—the incessant roar of the rifle; the screaming bullets; the forest on fire; men cheering, groaning, yelling, swearing and praying! All this created an experience in the minds of the survivors that we can never forget."[9]

A few days later, Billy Yank and Johnny Reb would again meet at the "Bloody Angle" at Spotsylvania, where Vermonter William Noyes would earn himself the Congressional Medal of Honor. In front of their position one of the Johnny Rebs raised a white rag attached to his musket. Accepting this as the traditional sign of truce, a Vermont soldier stood up to see what they wanted. He was met with a hail of bullets and killed. Union soldier Noyes was "infuriated beyond control by such treachery and determined upon revenge." He had his fellow soldiers all load their rifles, and then he jumped up on top of the

fortifications and began firing down into the Johnny Rebs as fast as he could be handed the loaded rifles. Amazingly he fired fifteen rifles and was not injured. He did note, trying to explain how he was not all that heroic, that "The enemy did not seem to regain their wits until I had fired five or six shots."[10]

The two armies raced south. Grant planned to take Petersburg, located 20 miles south of the Confederate capital at Richmond, and the hub of all the southern railroad lines. The Johnny Rebs arrived there before him in June 1864, and both sides began to dig in for a very different kind of war, one that would last for ten months. Billy Yank and Johnny Reb lived that time in fortified trenches that stretched from Petersburg to Richmond and engaged in artillery and sniper warfare with occasional attempts to break through the lines. Confederate soldier John Wise found life in the trenches "indescribably monotonous and uncomfortable." He found the heat on sunny days to be intense and rainy days found himself "ankle-deep in tough, clinging mud." With the army trenches only about two hundred yards apart in some places, there was constant danger. Wise

A MEMORIAL
TO THE
AFRICAN-
AMERICAN
SOLDIERS WHO
SERVED IN THE
CIVIL WAR WAS
UNVEILED
IN JULY 1998.

noted that because "both sides had attained accurate marksmanship . . . even the act of going to a spring for water involved risk of life or limb."[11]

Johnny Reb and Billy Yank actually became quite friendly at times during the long siege. Either side could call out for a truce during which they would talk or even exchange items. Wise notes that the truce would end "by some one calling out from the rifle-pits that orders had come to reopen fire at a designated time, sufficiently remote to allow everybody to seek cover."[12] And then the war would go on.

Sometimes when the war went on, it was quite spectacular. A Union plan to undermine the seigeworks at Petersburg by tunneling under them and filling the tunnel with explosives led to a particularly violent explosion and a devastating charge by a black regiment commanded by white officer Robert Beecham. Following orders after the explosion, the black troops marched into their assigned positions where, Beecham reports "The Confederates soon recovered from their confusion and concentrated their batteries upon us, catching us like sheep in a slaughter pen." Beecham himself was taken prisoner by the end of the battle, and the losses to his unit were large—one third killed, wounded, or missing. In the years after the war, when critics said that it was the black regiments that had failed to execute the Union plan, he strongly defended their actions that day: "The black boys formed promptly. There was no flinching on their part. They came to the shoulder touch [shoulder to shoulder] like true soldiers, as ready to face the enemy and meet death on the field as the bravest and best soldiers that ever lived."[13]

The war also continued in the Deep South as Sherman made his historic and devastating march to cut the Confederacy in half and stop the resupply of Virginia and its army. Several desperate attempts were also made by the Confederates to attack Washington, D.C., to draw off General Grant's troops from the siege at Petersburg. But overall, everyone seemed to know that the end was not far away. As Union engineer Thomas Owen wrote home on March 30, 1865: "The rebellion is in its last reel and, within the next few months, will fall prostrate before the victorious armies of the U.S."[14] The end was even closer than this Billy Yank thought.

Chapter 8
Heroes

"While carrying two case shots to the gun, having cut the fuse of one and made it ready be inserted, I was wounded by a piece of shell, which carried away my right arm at the shoulder, with a portion of the clavicle and scapula. So much of the shoulder was carried away that the cavity of the body was exposed, and the tissue of the lungs made plainly visible. It has been said by comrades who were at that gun as cannoneers that I inserted the shell into the gun after my arm was torn off, before I fell."[1] Private John Johnson, a Billy Yank from Wisconsin, gives this gruesome account of the injury he received at Fredericksburg, which earned him the Congressional Medal of Honor.

John Johnson was one of the small number (between 1,200 and 1,400) of Billy Yanks who earned this medal. The medal was awarded to Union soldiers who exhibited unusual bravery in battle conditions. Some years after the end of the Civil War, an effort was made to collect the stories of these medal winners. The resulting book, *Deeds of Valor*, gives a wonderful picture of the heroism of Billy Yank. Included are 230 stories of soldiers who risked their lives on the battlefield. Many of the stories tell of soldiers who braved enemy fire to rescue wounded friends. Many others tell of soldiers like John Johnson who, after being wounded themselves, continued to offer heroic service.

Some of the stories are even amusing. Private Delano J. Morey, an Ohio soldier retreating with other members of his company, saw two Confederate sharpshooters and charged at them alone as they loaded their guns to shoot him. The only problem with this was that his own gun was not loaded. That

THE MEDAL OF HONOR WAS AWARDED TO UNION SOLDIERS FOR EXCEPTIONAL BRAVERY IN BATTLE. IT IS THE HIGHEST U.S. MILITARY DECORATION.

Peter McAdams, an Irishman and a member of a Pennsylvania unit, begged his captain for the chance to return and bring a wounded soldier to safety behind the lines. When the captain gave permission, he went out onto the field "on a dead run and under heavy fire." As he reached his own lines carrying his friend on his shoulders, he was in for a surprise. "A number of rebel soldiers, perhaps twenty, who witnessed the incident from a position behind the fence, cheered as they observed me escape their fire with my burden and gain the lines of my regiment. Our own men returned the cheer."[3]

Another rescue, which earned Eldridge Robinson of Ohio the Medal of Honor, was much more scary. He and the other soldier involved reached their comrade, Price Worthington, who had been shot through the body. Robinson wrote of their attempt to return to their own lines: "We picked him up, and, amid a rain of bullets, of which one hit the wounded man in the leg, and many cut holes in our clothes, we reached the top of the hill, when the gunner of a battery about seventy-five yards in the rear of our line, taking us for

didn't stop him. Morey remembers "I was a little too quick for them. I leveled my empty gun at them and ordered them to surrender, which they promptly did, and I led the captives to my captain. I was sixteen years old, and each of my prisoners was old enough to be my father."[2]

the enemy, sent a shell so close to our heads that we were both thrown to the ground."[4]

Private John Chase from Maine rescued himself to earn the Medal of Honor. The story is an amazing one. Chase remembers: "One of those shrapnel shells exploded near me and forty-eight pieces of it entered my body. My right arm was shattered and my left eye was put out. I was carried a short distance to the rear as dead, and knew nothing more until two days after. When I regained consciousness, I was in a wagon with a lot of dead comrades being carted to the trenches to be buried. I moaned and called the attention of the driver, who came to my assistance."[5] When he finally arrived at the hospital, the doctors told him there was no hope. At one point the head surgeon told him he had less than six hours to live. But three months later Private Chase left that hospital to begin his recuperation and return home to Maine.

Several soldiers earned medals for defending the flags that were in their care as color-bearers. Sergeant William H. Carney, a member of the famous unit of black soldiers, the 54th Massachusetts, protected his flag in spite of enormous danger during the unit's attack on Fort Wagner: "In less than twenty minutes I found myself alone struggling upon the ramparts, while all around me lay the dead and wounded piled one upon another. As I could not go into the fort alone, I knelt down, still holding the flag in my hands. The musket balls and grape shot were flying all around me, and as they struck, the sand would fly in my face." Finally, he decided it was time to retreat and bring the colors to safety. "Upon rising to determine my course to the rear, I was struck by a bullet, but, as I was not prostrated by the shot, I continued my course. I had not gone very far, however, before I was struck by a second ball." A New York soldier had to help him now, but William Carney was determined to finish his task. "While on our way I was again wounded, this time in the head, and my rescuer then offered to carry the colors for me, but I refused to give them up, saying that no one but a member of my regiment should carry them." Finally arriving at the rear, he was proudest of the fact that "the old flag had never touched the ground."[6]

Private Martin Scheibner from Pennsylvania showed that a calm response can save a dangerous sit-

A ZOUAVE
AMBULANCE CREW
DEMONSTRATED HOW
TO REMOVE WOUNDED
SOLDIERS FROM THE
BATTLEFIELD.

51

uation and, in doing so, earned the Congressional Medal of Honor. A cannon shell landed in the middle of a group of soldiers from his unit with its fuse still burning. As everyone else scattered to get away from the shell before it exploded, Scheibner opened his canteen and poured his coffee on the burning fuse. The report on the incident notes that "The fuse had just about reached the shell" when his calm action saved them all from danger.[7]

The stories of these heroic Billy Yanks were saved for us because of the fact that they were awarded the Congressional Medal of Honor. No specific book of

52

stories of heroic deeds by Johnny Rebs exists. But there is no doubt that one could find as many heroic efforts among the Confederates as among the Union soldiers. One famous story illustrates their valor under fire.

During the horrible battle of Fredericksburg, Union troops made a number of assaults against Confederates in a secure position behind a stone wall. Many Union soldiers died on the field, but many others who were wounded had to stay on the field in the freezing December cold until the battle was over. They suffered horribly, and their cries for water caused a Confederate soldier to earn himself the title "the Angel of Marye's Heights." South Carolina soldier Richard Kirkland climbed over the wall while Union fire continued and brought water to the wounded Union soldiers suffering on the field. Today a statue near the stone wall honors his courageous actions in which he saw the wounded Union Billy Yanks not as enemies but as suffering human beings.

Chapter 9
Wounded

"Just as Major Spear received the order to retreat, I was wounded, a minie-ball passing through my left ankle. It is impossible to describe the sensations experienced by a person when wounded for the first time," wrote Billy Yank Theodore Gerrish. But even worse than being wounded was the situation in which Gerrish now found himself: "Our regiment was rapidly retreating, and the rebels as rapidly advancing. The forest trees around me were on fire, and the bullets were falling thick and fast. If I remained where I was, the most favorable result that I could hope for was captivity, which, in reality, would be worse than death by the bullet on the field."[1]

Gerrish wrote here of Billy Yank and Johnny Reb's greatest fear. Over and over again the accounts speak of this fear of being seriously wounded but not killed outright. The stories we read of soldiers risking their own deaths to bring their wounded friends back within their own lines reflects that fear. Soldiers knew that to be wounded and left on the battlefield in the care of the enemy was the worst possible fate. Although a Confederate officer, such as William Oates, commander of the 15th Alabama, could acknowledge that the wounded soldiers he had to leave behind on Little Round Top at Gettysburg "were as well cared for as any wounded soldiers in the hands of an enemy ever are," it was a grudging statement and only partly a compliment to the Union surgeons.[2]

The reality of war was that after a battle, the army that had won and held possession of the battlefield took care of their own wounded first, as one would expect. Once their own were cared for, they then provided care to their wounded enemy prisoners. But, in a battle such as Gettysburg, where the number of wounded soldiers far exceeded the availability of surgeons, that could mean several days later. In the case

WOUNDED CONFEDERATES AT CAMP LETTERMAN AT GETTYSBURG

of the wounded of the 15th Alabama, it was two or three days before the soldiers were assisted. Oates told of one soldier, who lay in the rain for two days: "He lay on his back, could not turn, and kept from drowning by putting his hat over his face."[3] This particular soldier survived his ordeal. Many others, desperately needing medical attention, would die on the fields before anyone was available to care for them.

Being wounded and remaining behind enemy lines also meant that if you recovered you were a prisoner of war. Both Billy Yank and Johnny Reb were right to fear being held prisoners of war by their enemies. But while their real fear was of being wounded and left behind, being wounded and remaining under their own army's care was often not much better.

After battle, the wounded soldiers who could manage to do so made their way back to field hospitals set up behind the battle lines. Those who could not leave the battlefield without help hoped

for friends to return for them or for the drummer boys, assigned as stretcher bearers, to get to them and bring them to the field hospital. There those who the surgeons felt could be treated received emergency care and then were transported away from the battlefield.

Transport from the battlefield to trains or hospital ships that would bring the soldiers to general hospitals was also a grueling experience. William Reed, who was involved with the Sanitary Commission providing care to the soldiers, described the "privi-lege" of ambulance transport away from the battle-field. "What a privilege!" he wrote. "A privilege of being violently tossed from side to side, of having one of the four who occupy the vehicle together thrown bodily, perhaps, upon a gaping wound; of being tor-tured, and racked, and jolted, when each jarring of the ambulance is enough to make the sympathetic brain burst with agony."[4]

As the war progressed, Billy Yanks and Johnny Rebs who made it off the battlefield and back to the general hospitals usually survived their injuries. This

SOLDIERS OF THE VETERAN
RESERVE CORPS STATIONED IN
ALEXANDRIA, VIRGINIA

was because the hospitals them-selves had improved and their staffs had learned more about what care would bring the best results. But survival, at a time when three out of every four surgeries done on the soldiers were amputations, meant long months of rehabilitation, learning how to cope with a prosthesis (an artificial limb that would replace an arm or a leg) and trying to get back to living a normal life.

Some soldiers had wounds that allowed them to return to their units to fight after they had recovered. Many Union soldiers who had moderately serious wounds but were no longer fit to fight still remained in the army, serving in the Veteran Reserve Corps that was founded in 1863. They served as guards, prisoner escorts, nurses, cooks—jobs normally done by uninjured soldiers who could be better used fighting Johnny Reb. Alfred Bellard, a New Jersey soldier, was wounded in the leg at the Battle of Chancellorsville in May 1863. His injury did not require amputation, but he was not considered recovered until October. He was not ruled fit to rejoin his regiment and instead was assigned to the Veteran Reserve Corps. Here he would spend the rest of the war still serving his country in spite of his wounds. And, along with the other members of the Corps, he would even have a chance to be a hero.

In July 1864 when Confederate General Jubal Early snuck up the Shenandoah Valley into Maryland and made a surprise attack on Fort Stevens outside of Washington, D.C., it was the Veteran Reserve Corps that held off the Confederate troops until reinforcements arrived from Grant's army in Virginia. They received a hero's welcome from the residents of Washington, Bellard noting that the residents "were glad to see the Regt. back again as they were well thought of for their efficiency and soldierly bearing."[5]

Let us return to Billy Yank Theodore Gerrish whose fearful situation began the chapter. He would recover, return to the 20th Maine, and fight until the end of the war. How he escaped his predicament is a tribute to his determination not to be left behind on the battlefield during the Wilderness Campaign. He forced himself to his feet and discovered that he could manage to run as long as he kept his leg perfectly straight. He wrote: "Fear lent wings to my flight, and away I dashed. Frequently my wounded leg would refuse to do good service, and as a result I would tumble headlong upon the ground, then rising, I would rush on again." Finally reaching the field hospital, he waited three days to have his wound cared for and then was transported to a hospital in a baggage wagon with twelve other soldiers. His memory of that time? "Those were terrible hours. How plainly they are pictured upon my mind!"[6]

Chapter 10
Prisoner of War

Remember the words of Billy Yank Theodore Gerrish as he considered his situation after being wounded: "If I remained where I was the most favorable result that I could hope for was captivity, which, in reality, would be worse than death."[1] Billy Yanks dreaded the thought of being imprisoned at places such as Andersonville, where 13,000 Union soldiers died, or Libby Prison in Richmond, where "the floors, walls, clothes, and the bodies of the men swarm with vermin," in the words of one Union soldier imprisoned there for several weeks.[2] Johnny Reb also feared the Union prisons. The one advantage that Johnny Reb had in being a Union prisoner was that the food was better and more readily available. As conditions in the South worsened, Billy Yanks in prison there also had to face starvation.

The life of the soldiers held as prisoners was truly horrible. But it is necessary to keep in mind the words of one historian: "Unpleasant as is the story of the prisons of the Civil War, however great their shortcomings, the treatment of prisoners . . . marks a decided advance over the general practice of the world before that time."[3]

There are rules that existed during the Civil War—and still exist in modern times—about how prisoners of war are to be treated. They have to be protected from harm; given a place to live; provided with food, clothing, and medical care if they need it; and supplied with other basic necessities, like bedding and fuel, to keep them alive and reasonably well. These rules are agreed upon by all nations. Unfortunately, during war, which is just when such rules are most needed, sometimes they are not followed as well as they should be.

The Civil War was even more complicated than most wars because it was not seen as a war between two countries but as a fight within one country. The

CONDITIONS FOR PRISONERS WERE OFTEN UNSANITARY. THE ONLY WATER AVAILABLE WAS USED FOR BATHING, WASHING CLOTHES, AND DRINKING.

Union tried to claim early in the war that prisoners taken in battle were not prisoners of war at all. Instead they were people who had committed treason against their country and should be killed. The Confederacy reacted by threatening to treat Billy Yanks the same way and kill them. Finally both sides agreed to follow the normal rules for prisoners of war.

The first problem both sides had was to find enough places to house all the prisoners who were being taken in battle. Historians still argue today over how many Civil War soldiers spent time as prisoners of war. One report says that there were about 211,000 Billy Yanks and 460,000 Johnny Rebs taken prisoner over the course of the Civil War.

The other serious problem was finding enough food and supplies to provide for them. Both governments were already struggling just trying to find enough room and supplies for their own armies. The Union and Confederate governments issued orders that their prisoners would be treated as well as their own soldiers. They would receive the same rations as regular soldiers and the same issue of supplies such as clothing. While these were the standards set for treating prisoners, the conditions that prisoners of war experienced during the Civil War were usually far worse.

At their worst, the conditions were almost unspeakable. The Confederate prison camp at Andersonville, Georgia, is remembered today as the most horrible of all the camps on either side. At one point in August 1864 this camp, built to hold 10,000 Union prisoners, held 33,000. The prisoners were not allowed to build shelters because there was not enough room, and they lived in holes they dug in the ground with their hands. Rations were scarce—according to one account, "a teaspoon of salt, three tablespoons of beans, and half a pint of unsifted corn-

meal." Even Southern observers felt pity for the conditions these Billy Yanks had to endure. Wrote one Southern woman, "My heart aches for these poor wretches, Yankees though they are, and I am afraid God will suffer some terrible retribution to fall upon us for letting such things happen."[4]

If Andersonville was the worst, the experiences of soldiers at other prison camps were not much better. Union Colonel John Coburn filed this official report on the treatment of his troops taken prisoner in Tennessee: "The men, shivering, half-starved, without sleep or rest, were then crowded into box-cars. . . . The floor of the one I was in was covered with wet manure. Thus we traveled that day to Chattanooga. On arriving there we were placed, without rations, for the night in a large frame house just erected for a hospital; crowded in, almost to suffocation."

Eventually transferred to Libby Prison in Richmond, Virginia, Colonel Coburn described their food as "half a pound a day of bread and of putrid, starveling meat, totally unfit for use, filling the room with a foul stench on being brought in."[5] Another Union prisoner confined at Libby Prison also spoke

UNION PRISONERS IN
THE OVERCROWDED
CONFEDERATE PRISON
CAMP AT ANDERSON-
VILLE HAD LITTLE TO
EAT AND MANY WERE
FORCED TO LIVE IN
HOLES IN THE GROUND.

of the terrible conditions there and added bitterly in his report: "I sincerely hope that rebel officers in our hands will be compelled to live on similar short allowances."[6]

There were similar complaints about conditions in the prisons in the Union. Secretary of State William Seward wrote to the secretary of war after being visited by the British consul (an embassy officer) in Philadelphia, who was filing a complaint

about the conditions of Confederate prisoners at Fort Delaware. The prison's walls were called "wet with moisture, the stone floor damp and cold, the air impure and deathly, no bed or couches to lie upon and offensive vermin crawling in every direction."[7]

Just as historians disagree about how many Union and Confederate soldiers were prisoners of war, they also disagree about how many of them died while in captivity. The best estimates are that 30,000 Billy

62

FORT DELAWARE HOUSED CONFEDERATE PRISONERS. THIS PHOTO SHOWS A LONG LINE OF PRISONERS ARRIVING FROM THEIR DEFEAT AT VICKSBURG.

Yanks and 26,000 Johnny Rebs died in captivity. There was a prisoner exchange program between the North and the South, but it worked less effectively as the war continued. One major problem occurred once black Union troops were taken prisoner after battles. President Jefferson Davis ordered that black prisoners be treated as "slaves in insurrection," and many were executed on the spot (300 of them in one instance, after the battle at Fort Pillow). Others were sold as slaves.

Hannah Johnson, the mother of a soldier in the 54th Massachusetts, wrote directly to Abraham Lincoln about the treatment of black prisoners, even though her son had not been taken prisoner: "I know that a colored man ought to run no greater risques [risks] than a white, his pay is no greater his obligation to fight is the same. So why should not our enemies be compelled to treat him the same. . . . Now Mr Lincoln dont you think you oght [ought] to stop this thing and make them do the same by the colored men. . . . We poor oppressed ones appeal to you, and ask fair play." When General Grant ordered that no prisoner exchanges would occur again until the South treated the black prisoners equally, the South refused and the prisoner exchange program ended.[8]

In light of the gruesome conditions and the very real risk of dying while serving time as a prisoner of war, it is no wonder that after being taken prisoner, so many soldiers tried to escape. One famous escape from Libby Prison occurred in February 1864. By then Libby Prison housed only Union officers, and they were carefully watched. One hundred and nine of them still managed a spectacular escape by crawling through a tunnel that they dug under the wall of the prison and that came out across the street. More would have escaped that night except they became too loud and their noise brought the guards. Forty-eight were recaptured and two drowned, but the rest made it to the Union lines.

As word got around about what the soldiers would have to face in prison, it is easy to understand why Theodore Gerrish and many other Billy Yanks and Johnny Rebs looked on being captured as being worse than death.

Chapter 11
Dealing with Death

"Without doubt, many not yet dead were buried alive, as we have reason to know from some who revived enough to protest, just as they were about to be placed in the pit. The usual way is not to dig a grave for each man, but a long pit about six and a half feet wide and deep enough to hold all the dead in the immediate vicinity. The bodies are placed side by side and on top of each other in the pit, which is then covered over much the same as farmers cover potatoes and roots to preserve them from the frost of winter; with this exception, however: the vegetables really get more tender care." This simple description of the burial of the dead after a battle comes from the memoirs of Father Corby, chaplain of the Irish Brigade. He added: "This is not an overdrawn picture, but one witnessed by hundreds of us during many battles."[1]

One of the hardest duties that faced Billy Yank and Johnny Reb after a battle was the burial of their dead. Billy Yank Theodore Gerrish wrote of the first time he saw a battlefield—this one covered with dead Confederate soldiers. It happened before he ever saw battle himself. "With a hushed voice and careful tread I passed over them, wondering if the time would come in the varying fortunes of war, when the enemy would thus pass over the bodies of our own regiment, lying lifeless and cold upon some bloody field."[2]

It is not hard to imagine what it must have been like to search the battlefield for soldiers who had been your friends and find them lying dead—then to have to carry them back and bury them in a common grave, knowing that it could have just as easily been you who had been killed in the battle. Many of the accounts of the soldiers speak of the deaths of friends

IN MANY CASES, THE DEAD WERE BURIED HURRIEDLY.
THE UNION DEAD SHOWN HERE WERE INTERRED IN
CASKETS, WHICH OFTEN WERE NOT READILY AVAILABLE.

who had premonitions before the battle that they would die. Union soldier William Lord described finding his friend, Private Reed, dead on the battlefield after the Battle at Drewry's Bluff in 1864: "Only the night before Reed told me that he felt as if he would be killed soon. 'If I am, Bill,' said he, 'go through my pockets and send the few belongings I have to my family.' There he was, poor fellow—dead! I stopped long enough to carry out his request."[3]

Elisha Rhodes of the 2nd Rhode Island tells of a soldier who "showed me a board on which he had carved his name, date of birth and had left a place for his date of death. . . . I asked him if he expected to be killed and he said no, and that he had made his head board only for fun."[4] The soldier was killed in the fighting near Petersburg the next day.

John Wise, one of the Virginia Military Institute cadets who gained fame at the Battle of New Market, wrote later that his roommate, Jack Stanard, had "confessed a presentiment that he would be killed" the night before the battle. Since both cadets had

66 been ordered to stay behind and guard the supply wagons, John Wise also felt guilty "for my part in drawing him into the fight" even though they had decided together to disobey their orders and join the battle. When it ended, he went searching for his roommate. But he was too late: "Stanard had breathed his last but a few moments before we reached the old farmhouse. . . . His body was still warm."[5] Wise, just seventeen years old and wounded himself, was left with the task of writing to Stanard's mother and telling her that her son Jack had "died at this post fighting gallantly for his country's cause."[6]

Perhaps what made dealing with death so real was that it was so commonplace. Since most regiments were formed from local communities, Billy Yank and Johnny Reb were usually fighting with their neighbors by their sides. After a battle, they were often the first bearers of bad tidings to the families of the soldiers killed in battle. They were the ones who delivered the last messages home, who told how the soldier had died, and gave what comfort they could. Reading the letters written by one individual over the

course of the war, one gets used to the constant litany of deaths. How hard it must have been for Billy Yank and Johnny Reb, never knowing whether the next letter home from someone in their regiment might be the one announcing his own death in battle.

The best description of what made Billy Yank and Johnny Reb able to deal with death as well as they did may be the one in a description of what it required to be a soldier, in the words of Johnny Reb Carlton McCarthy. "The dangers of the battle-field, and the demands upon his energy, strength, and courage, not only strengthen the old, but almost create new, faculties of mind and heart," he wrote. "The death, sudden and terrible, of those dear to him, the imperative necessity of standing to his duty while the wounded cry and groan . . . the terrible thirst, hunger, heat, and weariness—all these teach a boy self-denial, attachment to duty . . . and, instead of hardening him, . . . make him pity and love even the enemy of his country, who bleeds and dies for *his* country."[7]

Chapter 12
Finally, the End

Sunday, April 2, 1865, was "a perfect Sunday of the Southern spring," in the words of Richmond socialite Constance Cary Harrison. But while attending church, she saw a note handed to Confederate President Jefferson Davis. "I happened to sit in the rear of the President's pew," she wrote, "so near that I plainly saw the sort of gray pallor that came upon his face as he read."[1] The note, from General Robert E. Lee, said that the Petersburg siege was about to end. The Confederate army could no longer defend the Confederate capital at Richmond.

As the government pulled out of the capital, there was chaos. Confederate General Ewell made the decision to burn the supplies left in the city so they would not fall into Union hands. No one expected the disaster that resulted. LaSalle Pickett, wife of Confederate General George Pickett, was in Richmond on that fateful night. She remembered: "A breeze springing up suddenly from the south fanned the slowly flickering flames into a blaze . . . they were carried to the next building, and the next. . . . Still the flames raged on. They leaped from house to house in mad revel."[2]

On the morning of April 3, 1865, Union soldiers marched into Richmond and replaced the Confederate flag flying over the state capital with the Stars and Stripes. Billy Yanks had spent the last four years trying to march into Richmond and at last they were there. Abraham Lincoln himself visited the city the next day and walked the streets to the Confederate White House and sat at Jefferson Davis's desk. Everyone knew that it was just a matter of time until the war would be over.

Only some of the Billy Yanks had the honor of occupying Richmond. Most of them, after the long siege of Petersburg, were back on the march again,

BEFORE RICHMOND FELL TO FEDERAL TROOPS, THE CONFEDERATES SET FIRE TO ANYTHING OF MILITARY VALUE, SUCH AS THIS RAILROAD BRIDGE. THE FIRE SPREAD AND DESTROYED A GOOD PART OF THE CITY.

chasing after the Johnny Rebs of the Army of Northern Virginia, hoping for one final confrontation. General Lee had split his retreating army into two sections and ordered both to march to the town of Amelia Court House, about 35 miles away, where supplies were waiting for them. Lieutenant John Wise was sent to deliver a message to General Lee and came upon the main body of the retreating Confederates. He wrote: "How they straggled, and how demoralized they seemed!"[3]

General Grant's objective was to stop Lee's army from reaching their supplies. But the Billy Yanks could not stop the rebels before they reached Amelia Court House—not that it ended up mattering at all, because only ammunition had arrived. By now the Johnny Rebs were starving, and ammunition was not what General Lee needed to keep his army on the march. Johnny Reb Carlton McCarthy records that all that was left was the "corn on the cob intended for the horses. Two ears were issued to each man. It was parched in the coals, mixed with salt, stored in the pockets, and eaten on the road. Chewing the corn was hard work . . . it made the jaw ache and the gums and the teeth so sore as to cause almost unendurable pain."[4] But it was all the food they would get.

The Billy Yanks sensed that the end was near and they were overjoyed. Dr. Alfred Woodhull remembered: "We were like so many schoolboys on a holiday . . . the spirit of prophecy within us announced that the day of retribution for the wicked Rebels was at hand, that we were surely crushing the rebellion."[5]

But the end was not quite yet, and more Billy Yanks and Johnny Rebs would die in one last battle when the armies met at Sayler's Creek on April 6. It began with small skirmishes, and for Johnny Reb Carlton McCarthy it was an exhausting final battle. "The race to the top of the long hill was exceedingly trying to men already exhausted by continual marching, hunger, thirst, and loss of sleep. They ran, panting for breath, like chased animals, fairly staggering as they went."[6] A large portion of the Army of Northern Virginia was captured at the Battle of Sayler's Creek. When the battle was over, the remainder of the Confederate army continued its retreat, marching toward the small town of Appomattox Court House, where it would all end.

General Grant had begun a correspondence with General Lee during the retreat. He wrote to him on April 7: "The results of the last week must convince you of the hopelessness of further resistance." He wanted to end the "further effusion of blood" and asked Lee to surrender. Lee replied the next day,

declining to surrender now, but asking what terms of surrender Grant would be willing to offer. Grant's answering letter was generous and sympathetic, with no hint of a gloating victor. "Peace being my great desire, there is but one condition I would insist upon, namely, that the men and officers surrendered shall be disqualified for taking up arms again."[7]

On Palm Sunday, April 9, 1865, General Grant and General Lee met in the parlor of the home of Wilmer McLean in Appomattox Court House. The next day General Lee sent his General Order No. 9, which ordered the Johnny Rebs to "return to their homes," assuring them of his "unceasing admiration of your constancy and devotion to your country."[8] More important for the starving Confederates was their first meal as a defeated army. Carlton McCarthy wrote: "A line of men came single file over the hill near the camp, each bearing on his shoulder a box of 'hard-tack' or crackers. Behind these came a beef, driven by soldiers. The crackers and beef were a present from the Federal [Union] troops near, who, knowing the famished condition of the surrounded army, had contributed their day's rations for its relief."[9]

71

GENERAL LEE
LEAVING THE
MCLEAN HOUSE
AFTER SURRENDER-
ING, APRIL 9, 1865

Billy Yank Theodore Gerrish was also there at Appomattox. He wrote of his feelings toward the now-defeated enemy: "All of our associations with the rebels at Appomattox were of the most pleasant character. Great care was taken by our soldiers not to wound their feelings, and they exhibited their grati-tude by many pleasant words. . . . They had lost all by the war, but they accepted the situation gracefully."[10]

Three days later, on April 12, 1865, the formal "passing of the armies" took place. The Confederate soldiers passed in review and then stacked their arms and turned in their flags. It was a difficult moment for both sides. The Johnny Rebs were admitting defeat and that was a humiliating thing to have to do after four long years of war. The Billy Yanks had a difficult job also. These were their fellow citizens they were welcoming back into their country. There could be no gloating that they had won.

General Grant appointed General Joshua Lawrence Chamberlain to conduct the passing of the armies. The two men shared the view that the moment should be a solemn one, and one that recognized the courage of the defeated Confederates. So Chamberlain ordered silence as the defeated troops passed by, and then had the Union soldiers salute their former enemy. Theodore Gerrish remembered:

"Our commander, with the true courtesy of a chivalrous spirit, gave the command 'Shoulder arms,' and we thus saluted our fallen enemies. They returned the salute."[11] It was a moment of reconciliation for Johnny Reb and Billy Yank.

There had also been a very touching and significant moment at the actual signing of the surrender by Confederate General Robert E. Lee. Lt. Colonel Ely Parker, a Seneca Indian from New York and a member of General Grant's staff, was introduced to General Lee by General Grant. General Lee commented "I am glad to see one real American." Parker answered: "We are all Americans."[12] Indeed, with the war now over, we finally were.

Chapter 13
Changed
Forever

With the war over, Billy Yank and Johnny Reb returned to their real lives at home. But in some ways they never left the war behind them. Going home would be, of course, a very different experience for Johnny Reb than it was for Billy Yank. Following the surrender ceremony at Appomattox Court House, the Johnny Rebs headed for home, not knowing what they would find. Because most of the fighting of the Civil War had been done in Southern territory, the first work of most of the Johnny Rebs would be the rebuilding of their homes and communities.

Carlton McCarthy and a friend of his headed for Richmond. They had heard that "some young confederates, who were smart, were at work in the ruins cleaning bricks at five dollars a day. Others had government work, as clerks, mechanics, and laborers, earning from one to five dollars a day."[1] Of course,

they would be required to take a loyalty oath to the federal government before they could get a job.

But for the most part, the Johnny Rebs accepted that the war was over and that they had lost, though they had fought long and hard. Although many of the officers of the Confederate army would return home to continue debating the war for the rest their lives, the common Johnny Rebs were more than willing to go on with their lives.

Billy Yank received a hero's welcome at the end of the war. On May 23 and 24, 1865, 150,000 soldiers of the Union army marched in the Grand Review of the Armies in Washington, D.C. Theodore Gerrish felt that the review "reminded us of the histories we had studied in our school days, about the armies of Rome marching in grand processions and carrying the sacred eagles through the Eternal City." He was pleased to have the opportunity to "march through

AT THE END OF THE WAR, VICTORIOUS UNION TROOPS PASSED IN REVIEW IN WASHINGTON, D.C.

the streets of the capital of the great Western Republic, amid scenes as magnificent and with steps as haughty, as those of the old Roman soldiers in the days of their pride and power."[2]

The Grand Review completed, the various units were sent back to their home states to be mustered out. Returning home, they did not have to face a devastated landscape as did the Johnny Rebs. Most had left their homes as young boys. They came back as men, married their sweethearts, and returned to leading their normal lives. But they did face a changed world, and in many ways, the war stayed with them.

The Civil War brought with it great technological change. There were the obvious improvements in weaponry that come with all wars.

A NUMBER OF NORTHERN AND SOUTHERN WOMEN WERE NURSES DURING THE WAR. OTHERS WORKED IN FACTORIES OR SMUGGLED INFORMATION.

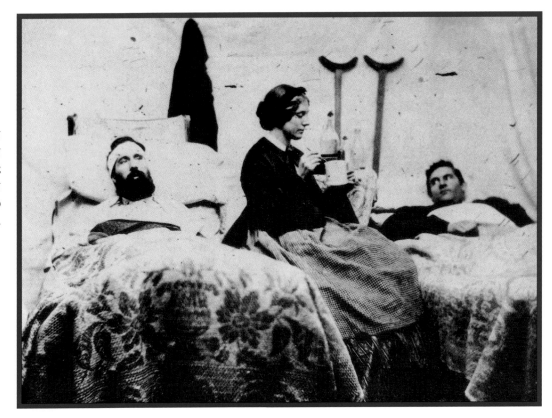

There were great changes in the practice of medicine that came from treating the soldiers who suffered from disease or from wounds during the Civil War. But the Civil War also brought with it societal changes, mostly in the role of women. During the Civil War, wives had been left at home to not only raise the children but also to run the farms. In addition, women had been given the opportunity to aid in the care of sick and wounded soldiers. For a good number of these women, there was to be no return to the ways of the past. They liked the independence that having their men at war had given them, and they intended to keep it. It would not be long before they used that new independence to try to give themselves a larger role in society.

Many of the soldiers who returned home were left with injuries that did not allow them to continue to perform the jobs they had left behind when they joined the army. Three-quarters of the injuries during the Civil War had been to arms or legs, and three-quarters of those injuries had resulted in amputation. For these soldiers, their wounds would change the plans they had to return home and pick up where they had left off at the beginning of the war.

Another interesting societal effect came from the fact that many of the soldiers who would never have traveled more than a few miles from their home if they had not gone off to war now found that they wished to see more of the world. The restlessness of the returning soldiers fueled the westward expansion and helped to populate the vast Western Territories.

No matter where they went, both Billy Yank and Johnny Reb kept the memory of the Civil War alive. Rutherford B. Hayes served in the Civil War with the 23rd Ohio Infantry. He later was elected president of the United States. One would think that being elected president would be the high point of anyone's career, but for Hayes his experience in what he called "the glorious war" was the memory that he most treasured. Right up to the end of his life he would maintain that "The war years were the best years of our lives."[3]

Johnny Reb Carlton McCarthy had a similar view. He noted "no country likes to part with a good earnest war. It likes to talk about the war, write its history, fight its battles over and over again, and build monument after monument to commemorate its glories."[4] Billy Yank Theodore Gerrish felt the same way: "We gather in our Grand Army Halls, to fight our battles over again, to sing the old patriotic songs once more, and under that inspiration, to reform our ranks. . . . We derive satisfaction from that."[5]

Billy Yanks organized themselves into groups to remember their glorious past. There were the Grand Army of the Republic, the Military Order of the Loyal Legion of the United States, and for their children, the Sons of Union Veterans. For Johnny Rebs, there were the United Confederate Veterans and countless other organizations, and for Southern women, the Daughters of the Confederacy. The soldiers organized themselves into Camp Fires to share stories of their adventures; they wrote articles for such publications as the *Confederate Veteran*; they visited the sites of their battles; and, in so doing, kept the war alive in their minds and in their hearts.

IN 1910, CONFEDERATE VETERANS GATHERED IN VIRGINIA TO REMEMBER THE WAR.

In July 1913, more than 53,000 Billy Yanks and Johnny Rebs returned to the site of the most famous battle of the Civil War— Gettysburg. On July 3 soldiers who had participated in Pickett's Charge both as Billy Yanks and Johnny Rebs faced each other on the same ground. One observer of the reenactment wrote of the excitement as the waiting Billy Yanks scrambled across the wall to meet their oncoming foes. "The emotion of the moment was so contagious that there was scarcely a dry eye in the huge throng."[6] Amazingly, in 1938, more than 1,800 Billy Yanks and Johnny Rebs returned to celebrate the seventy-fifth anniversary of the battle. Most of the men were now in their nineties; some were even over one hundred years old. Although the war was seventy-five years in the past, what lingered was not the horror of the battles that had divided them but rather the shared experience that now united them.

One would think that with the Civil War having ended so many years ago, by now we would only read about it in history books. In fact, thousands of men (estimates are as many as 30,000) routinely spend their weekends reenacting the lives of Billy Yank and

IN 1913, BILLY YANKS AND JOHNNY REBS HELD A GREAT REUNION IN GETTYSBURG. IN 1938, A LAST HANDFUL OF VETERANS HELD ONE LAST REUNION THERE.

Johnny Reb. They carefully search for any detail that will make the experience more real. It is not unusual to hear a reenactor speak excitedly about finding new information giving detailed instructions on the correct placement of uniform badges. The reenactors wear the same scratchy wool uniforms, eat the same food, and live as closely as possible under the same conditions as the Civil War soldiers. In the words of Civil War historian and veteran reenactor Brian Pohanka: "As one who has been involved in Civil War living history for twenty years, I have found it a great learning experience. When I read soldiers' accounts I can now apply some sense of what they are describing in the way of drill, tactics, the smell of gunpowder, the heft of musket and knapsack, the cold nights or hot days, the campfire and welcome tin cup of coffee, the camaraderie of my 'pards' . . . it is a way to bridge the centuries . . ."[7]

80 FOR A BRIEF TIME, REENACTORS REMEMBER THE CIVIL WAR. THEN THEY PUT DOWN THEIR WEAPONS, PACK UP THEIR GEAR, AND GO HOME. THE REAL WAR IS LONG OVER.

In staging reenactments, these new-day Billy Yanks and Johnny Rebs keep the Civil War alive for all of us to see as we visit battlefield sites and watch their demonstrations of how the soldiers lived, how their weapons fired, and what their daily lives were like. There is no way, of course, for reenactors to capture the confusion of battle, the nightmare of finding one's friends dead on the field, the actual horrors that Billy Yank and Johnny Reb experienced.

The Civil War is long over. Every Billy Yank and every Johnny Reb is long dead. But something of their story seems to call to us from the past. And as long as it does, Billy Yank and Johnny Reb will never die. Theodore Gerrish knew it would be so: "The country will always honor our memory, and not forget us when we have vanished from its sight. Our graves will not be neglected when there are no Grand Army comrades to scatter their floral offerings upon them."[8]

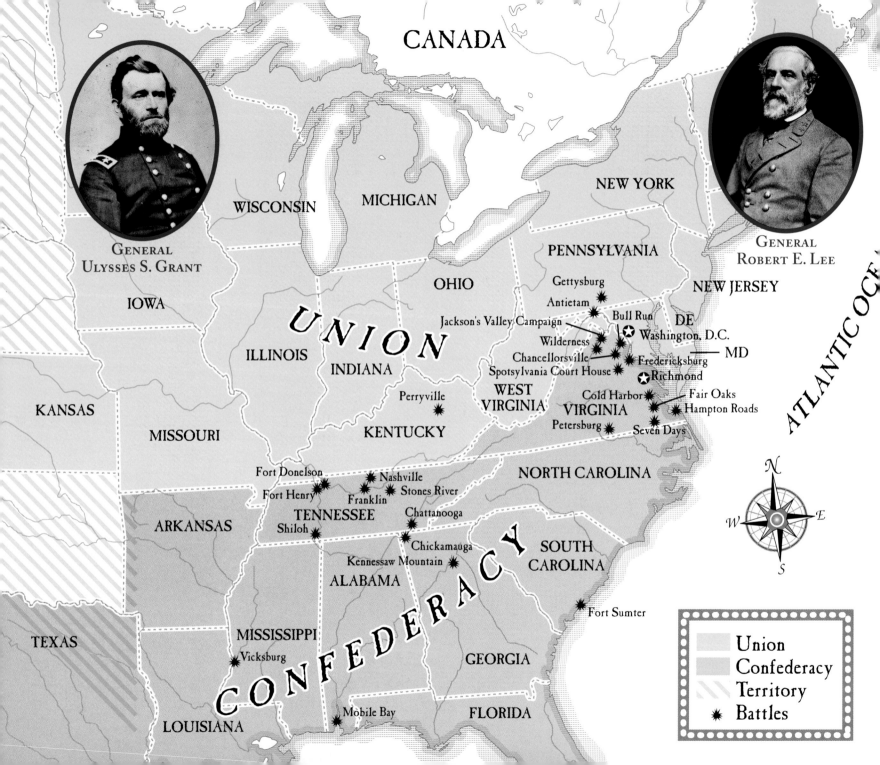

CANADA

GENERAL
Ulysses S. Grant

GENERAL
Robert E. Lee

WISCONSIN

MICHIGAN

NEW YORK

PENNSYLVANIA

NEW JERSEY

OHIO

Gettysburg

Antietam

IOWA

UNION

Jackson's Valley Campaign   Bull Run   DE

Wilderness   Washington, D.C.

Chancellorsville   MD

Spotsylvania Court House   Fredericksburg

ILLINOIS   INDIANA

Richmond

WEST
VIRGINIA   Cold Harbor   Fair Oaks

KANSAS   Perryville   VIRGINIA   Hampton Roads

MISSOURI   KENTUCKY   Petersburg   Seven Days

Fort Donelson   Nashville   NORTH CAROLINA

Fort Henry   Stones River

Franklin

ARKANSAS   TENNESSEE   Chattanooga   SOUTH
CAROLINA

Shiloh

Chickamauga

Kennessaw Mountain

ALABAMA

ATLANTIC OCE

N
W   E
S

TEXAS   MISSISSIPPI   Fort Sumter

Vicksburg   GEORGIA

CONFEDERACY

LOUISIANA   Mobile Bay   FLORIDA

Union
Confederacy
Territory
Battles

Chronology of the Civil War

November 6, 1860	Abraham Lincoln elected President of the United States
December 20, 1860	South Carolina secedes from the Union
February 18, 1861	Jefferson Davis inaugurated as President of the Confederate States of America
March 4, 1861	Abraham Lincoln inaugurated as President of the United States of America
April 12, 1861	Southern cannons fire on Fort Sumter and the conflict begins
April 19, 1861	President Lincoln orders a blockade of Southern ports
May 21, 1861	Richmond, Virginia, chosen as the capital of the Confederacy
July 21, 1861	Battle of Manassas (Bull Run)
February 16, 1862	Fort Donelson falls to Union troops
April 6–7, 1862	Battle of Shiloh
May–July 1862	Peninsula Campaign, ending with the Seven Days Battle
August 29–30, 1862	Second Battle of Manassas (Bull Run)
September 17, 1862	Battle of Antietam
December 13, 1862	Battle of Fredericksburg
December 31, 1862– January 2, 1863	Battle of Stones River

January 1, 1863	Emancipation Proclamation takes effect
May 1–4, 1863	Battle of Chancellorsville
July 1–3, 1863	Battle of Gettysburg
July 4, 1863	Vicksburg, Mississippi, siege ends with surrender of Confederates
July 18, 1863	Battle of Fort Wagner
September 19–20, 1863	Battle of Chickamauga
November 19, 1863	President Lincoln delivers the Gettysburg Address
November 23–25, 1863	Battle of Chattanooga
May 5–6, 1864	Battle of the Wilderness
May 8–19, 1864	Battle of Spotsylvania
September 2, 1864	Capture of Atlanta
November–December, 1864	Sherman's March to the Sea
June 20, 1864–April 2, 1865	Siege of Petersburg
April 3, 1865	Union troops enter the Confederate capital at Richmond
April 9, 1865	General Lee surrenders to General Grant at Appomattox Court House
April 14, 1865	Abraham Lincoln is assassinated at Ford's Theatre in Washington, D.C.

Source Notes

PROLOGUE

1. George Barton, Letter of May 19, 1864, quoted in Warren Wilkinson, *Mother, May You Never See the Sights I Have Seen* (New York: William Morrow, 1990), p. 121.

CHAPTER 1

1. Carlton McCarthy, *Detailed Minutiae of Soldier Life in the Army of Northern Virginia, 1861–1865* (Richmond; Carlton McCarthy and Company, 1882), p. 9.
2. Bell Irvin Wiley, *The Life of Billy Yank* (New York: Doubleday & Company, Inc., 1952), p. 299.
3. Geoffrey C. Ward. *The Civil War* (New York: Alfred A. Knopf, Inc., 1990), p. 248.
4. Ward, p. 253.
5. Thomas B. Allen. *The Blue and the Gray* (Washington, D.C.: National Geographic Society, 1992), p. 167.
6. *War of the Rebellion: A Compilation of the Official Records of the Union and Confederate Armies* (Washington, D.C.: Government Printing Office, 1890–1901), Series 1 Vol. XXVII, p. 378.
7. Sarah Rosetta Wakeman, *An Uncommon Soldier* (New York: Oxford University Press, 1994), pp. 28, 44.
8. Theodore Gerrish, *Army Life: A Private's Reminiscences of the Civil War* (Portland, Maine: Hoyt, Fogg & Donham, 1882), p. 15.
9. McCarthy, p. 193.

CHAPTER 2

1. Oliver W. Norton, *Army Letters 1861–1865* (Chicago: O. L. Deming, 1903), p. 28.
2. Theodore Gerrish, *Army Life: A Private's Reminiscences of the Civil War* (Portland, Maine: Hoyt, Fogg & Donham, 1882), p. 19.
3. Stephen B. Oates, *With Malice Toward None* (New York: New American Library, 1977), p. 271.
4. John Macdonald, *Great Battles of the Civil War* (New York: Collier Books, 1988), p. 12.

86

5. *War of the Rebellion: A Compilation of the Official Records of the Union and Confederate Armies* (Washington, D.C.: Government Printing Office, 1890–1901), Series 1 Vol. II, p. 316.

6. Henry N. Blake, "Bull Run: A Union Soldier," in Don Congdon, *Combat: The Civil War* (New York: Mallard Press, 1967), p. 27.

7. John W. Haley, *The Rebel Yell & the Yankee Hurrah* (Camden, Maine: Down East Books, 1985), p. 28.

8. Carlton McCarthy, *Detailed Minutiae of Soldier Life in the Army of Northern Virginia, 1861–1865* (Richmond; Carlton McCarthy and Company, 1882), p. 29.

9. Gerrish, p. 45.

10. Ibid.

11. McCarthy, p. 39.

12. Gerrish, p. 45.

CHAPTER 3

1. Carlton McCarthy, *Detailed Minutiae of Soldier Life in the Army of Northern Virginia, 1861–1865* (Richmond; Carlton McCarthy and Company, 1882), p. 31.

2. Dale E. Floyd, *The Letters and Diary of Thomas James Owen, Fiftieth New York Volunteer Engineer Regiment,*

During the Civil War (Washington, D.C.: U.S. Government Printing Office, 1985), pp. 5, 19, 22.

3. McCarthy, pp. 80–81.

4. McCarthy, p. 86.

5. Peter Welsh, *Irish Green and Union Blue* (New York: Fordham University Press, 1986), p. 41.

6. McCarthy, p. 92.

7. Theodore Gerrish, *Army Life: A Private's Reminiscences of the Civil War* (Portland, Maine: Hoyt, Fogg & Donham, 1882), p. 136.

8. Elisha Hunt Rhodes, *All for the Union* (New York: Orion Books, 1985), p. 218.

9. Welsh, p. 33.

10. Gerrish, p. 68.

11. Ira Berlin, ed. *Freedom's Soldiers: The Black Military Experience in the Civil War* (Cambridge, United Kingdom: Cambridge University Press, 1998), p. 117.

CHAPTER 4

1. Alfred Bellard, *Gone for a Soldier* (Boston: Little, Brown and Company, 1975), p. 118.

2. Carlton McCarthy, *Detailed Minutiae of Soldier Life in the Army of Northern Virginia, 1861–1865* (Rich-

mond; Carlton McCarthy and Company, 1882), p. 56.

3. William Bircher, *A Drummer-Boy's Diary: Comprising Four Years of Service with the Second Regiment Minnesota Veteran Volunteers, 1861 to 1865* (St. Paul: St. Paul Book and Stationery Company, 1889), p. 73.

4. Arthur W. Bergeron Jr. *The Civil War Reminiscences of Major Silas T. Grisamore, C.S.A.* (Baton Rouge: Louisiana State University Press, 1993), p. 66.

CHAPTER 5

1. William Corby, *Memoirs of Chaplain Life: Three Years with the Irish Brigade in the Army of the Potomac* (Notre Dame, Indiana: Scholastic Press, 1894), pp. 40–41.

2. Theodore Gerrish, *Army Life: A Private's Reminiscences of the Civil War* (Portland, Maine: Hoyt, Fogg & Donham, 1882), p. 49.

3. Austin Flint, M.D., ed. *Contributions Relating to the Causation and Prevention of Disease and to Camp Diseases* (New York: U.S. Sanitary Commission, 1867), p. 8.

4. Gerrish, p. 47.

5. James G. Hollandsworth Jr. *The Louisiana Native Guards: The Black Military Experience during the Civil War* (Baton Rouge: Louisiana State University Press, 1995), p. 98.

6. Corby, p. 41.

7. Corby, p. 41.

8. Albert T. Goodloe, "The Grayback was an Undisputed Success," in Rod Gregg, *The Illustrated Confederate Reader* (New York: Gramercy Books, 1989), p. 32–33.

CHAPTER 6

1. Theodore Gerrish, *Army Life: A Private's Reminiscences of the Civil War* (Portland, Maine: Hoyt, Fogg & Donham, 1882), p. 20.

2. Jaqueline Beverly Stanard, Letter to Mother, May 12, 1864. Stanard Papers, Preston Library, Virginia Military Institute.

3. Carlton McCarthy, *Detailed Minutiae of Soldier Life in the Army of Northern Virginia, 1861–1865* (Richmond; Carlton McCarthy and Company, 1882), p. 45.

4. John H. Worsham, "Marching Along at a Brisk Rate," in Rod Gregg, *The Illustrated Confederate Reader* (New York: Gramercy Books, 1989), p. 28.

5. Gerrish, p. 25.

88

6. William Corby, *Memoirs of Chaplain Life: Three Years with the Irish Brigade in the Army of the Potomac* (Notre Dame, Indiana: Scholastic Press, 1894), pp. 34–35.
7. George F. Williams, *Bullet and Shell* (New York: Fords, Howard, & Hulbert, 1884), p. 199.
8. McCarthy, p. 55.

CHAPTER 7

1. Elisha Hunt Rhodes, *All for the Union* (New York: Orion Books, 1985), p. 26.
2. William C. Davis, *Battle at Bull Run* (New York: Doubleday & Company, Inc., 1977), p. 178.
3. Sam R. Watkins, *Co. Aytch: A Side Show of the Big Show* (New York: Collier, 1962), p. 42.
4. John T. Bell, *Tramps and Triumphs of the Second Iowa Infantry* (Omaha: Gibson, Miller & Richardson, 1886), p. 17.
5. George F. Williams, *Bullet and Shell* (New York: Fords, Howard, & Hulbert, 1884), p. 98.
6. Stephen W. Sears, *Landscape Turned Red* (New York: Warner Books, 1983), p. 233.
7. William Corby, *Memoirs of Chaplain Life: Three Years with the Irish Brigade in the Army of the Potomac* (Notre Dame, Indiana: Scholastic Press, 1894), p. 132.
8. *Deeds of Valor: How America's Civil War Heroes Won the Medal of Honor* (Detroit, Michigan: Perrien-Keydel Co., 1903), p. 240.
9. Theodore Gerrish, *Army Life: A Private's Reminiscences of the Civil War* (Portland, Maine: Hoyt, Fogg & Donham, 1882), p. 162.
10. *Deeds of Valor*, p. 334.
11. John S. Wise, *The End of an Era* (Boston: Houghton, Mifflin and Company, 1901), p. 346.
12. Wise, p. 349.
13. Robert K. Beecham, *As If It Were Glory* (Madison, Wisconsin: Madison House, 1998), pp. 183, 184.
14. Dale E. Floyd, *The Letters and Diary of Thomas James Owen, Fiftieth New York Volunteer Engineer Regiment, During the Civil War* (Washington, D.C.: U.S. Government Printing Office, 1985), p. 80.

CHAPTER 8

1. *Deeds of Valor: How America's Civil War Heroes Won the Medal of Honor* (Detroit, Michigan: Perrien-Keydel Co., 1903), p. 115.
2. *Deeds of Valor*, p. 32.

3. *Deeds of Valor*, p. 148.
4. *Deeds of Valor*, p. 214.
5. *Deeds of Valor*, p. 159.
6. *Deeds of Valor*, pp. 258–259.
7. *Deeds of Valor*, p. 293.

CHAPTER 9

1. Theodore Gerrish, *Army Life: A Private's Reminiscences of the Civil War* (Portland, Maine: Hoyt, Fogg & Donham, 1882), pp. 166–167.
2. William C. Oates, *The War Between the Union and the Confederacy* (New York: The Neale Publishing Company, 1905), p. 226.
3. Oates, p. 227.
4. William Howell Reed, *Hospital Life in the Army of the Potomac* (Boston: William V. Spencer, 1866), p. 57.
5. Alfred Bellard, *Gone for a Soldier* (Boston: Little, Brown and Company, 1975), p. 275.
6. Gerrish, p. 169.

CHAPTER 10

1. Theodore Gerrish, *Army Life: A Private's Reminiscences of the Civil War* (Portland, Maine: Hoyt, Fogg & Donham, 1882), pp. 166–167.

2. William D. Wilkins, "Forgotten in the 'Black Hole': A Diary from Libby Prison," *Civil War Times Illustrated*, June 1976, p. 37.
3. Holland Thompson, ed. *The Photographic History of the Civil War*, Reprinted by The Blue and Grey Press, 1987 (c. 1911) Volume IV, Section 2 (Prisons and Hospitals), p. 14.
4. Geoffrey Ward, *The Civil War: An Illustrated History* (New York: Knopf, 1990), p. 338.
5. *War of the Rebellion: A Compilation of the Official Records of the Union and Confederate Armies* (Washington, D.C.: Government Printing Office, 1890–1901), Series I Vol. XXIII, pp. 92–93.
6. *War of the Rebellion*, Series II Vol. VIII, p. 337.
7. *War of the Rebellion*, Series II Vol. V, p. 216.
8. Ira Berlin, ed. *Freedom's Soldiers: The Black Military Experience in the Civil War* (Cambridge, United Kingdom: Cambridge University Press, 1998), pp. 106–108.

CHAPTER 11

1. William Corby, *Memoirs of Chaplain Life: Three Years with the Irish Brigade in the Army of the Potomac* (Notre Dame, Indiana: Scholastic Press, 1894), pp. 190–191, 192.

90

2. Theodore Gerrish, *Army Life: A Private's Reminiscences of the Civil War* (Portland, Maine: Hoyt, Fogg & Donham, 1882), p. 28.

3. *Deeds of Valor: How America's Civil War Heroes Won the Medal of Honor* (Detroit, Michigan: Perrien-Keydel Co., 1903), p. 343.

4. Elisha Hunt Rhodes, *All for the Union* (New York: Orion Books, 1985), p. 164.

5. John S. Wise, *The End of an Era* (Boston: Houghton, Mifflin and Company, 1901), p. 307.

6. John S. Wise, Letter to Mrs. Ellen Bankhead Stanard, May 19, 1864. Stanard Papers, Preston Library, Virginia Military Institute.

7. Carlton McCarthy, *Detailed Minutiae of Soldier Life in the Army of Northern Virginia, 1861–1865* (Richmond; Carlton McCarthy and Company, 1882), pp. 211–212.

CHAPTER 12

1. Mrs. Burton Harrison [Constance Cary], *Recollections, Grave and Gay* (New York: Charles Scribner's Sons, 1911), p. 207.

2. LaSalle Corbell Pickett, *Pickett and His Men* (Atlanta: Foote & Davies Company, 1899), p. 2.

3. John S. Wise, *The End of an Era* (Boston: Houghton, Mifflin and Company, 1901), p. 427.

4. Carlton McCarthy, *Detailed Minutiae of Soldier Life in the Army of Northern Virginia, 1861–1865* (Richmond; Carlton McCarthy and Company, 1882), p. 128.

5. Richard Wheeler, *Witness to Appomattox* (New York: HarperCollins Publishers, 1989), p. 148.

6. McCarthy, p. 140.

7. *War of the Rebellion: A Compilation of the Official Records of the Union and Confederate Armies* (Washington, D.C.: Government Printing Office, 1890–1901), Series 1 Vol. XLVI/Pt. 1, p. 56.

8. *War of the Rebellion*, Series 1 Vol. XLVI/Pt. 1, p. 1267.

9. McCarthy, p. 153.

10. Theodore Gerrish, *Army Life: A Private's Reminiscences of the Civil War* (Portland, Maine: Hoyt, Fogg & Donham, 1882), p. 266.

11. Gerrish, p. 261.

12. Thomas B. Allen. *The Blue and the Gray* (Washington, D.C.: National Geographic Society, 1992), p. 167.

CHAPTER 13

1. Carlton McCarthy, *Detailed Minutiae of Soldier Life in the Army of Northern Virginia, 1861–1865* (Richmond;

Carlton McCarthy and Company, 1882), p. 191.

2. Theodore Gerrish, *Army Life: A Private's Reminiscences of the Civil War* (Portland, Maine: Hoyt, Fogg & Donham, 1882), pp. 298–299.

3. Peggy Robbins, "The Glory Years," *Civil War Times Illustrated*, September/October 1994, p. 55.

4. McCarthy, p. 193.

5. Gerrish, p. 369.

6. James W. Wensyel, "Return to Gettysburg," *American History Illustrated*, July/August 1993, p. 50.

7. Brian Pohanka, Letter to the author, March 3, 1999.

8. Gerrish, p. 371.

For Further Information

BOOKS

Beller, Susan Provost. *Medical Practices in the Civil War*. Charlotte, VT: OurStory, 1992.

Brill, Marlene Targ. *Diary of a Drummer Boy*. Brookfield, CT: The Millbrook Press, 1998.

Egger-Bovet, Howard. *Book of the American Civil War*. Boston: Little, Brown & Co., 1998.

Gay, Kathlyn. *The Civil War*. Voices from the Past. Brookfield, CT: Twenty-First Century Books, 1995.

Murphy, Jim. *The Boy's War*. New York: Clarion Books, 1993.

Paulsen, Gary. *Soldier's Heart: Being the Story of the Enlistment and Due Service of the Boy Charley Goddard in the First Minnesota Volunteers*. New York: Delacorte, 1998.

Ray, Delia. *Behind the Blue and Gray*. New York: Puffin Books, 1996.

Reef, Catherine. *Civil War Soldiers*. Brookfield, CT: Twenty-First Century Books, 1993.

Robertson, James I., Jr. *Civil War! America Becomes One Nation*. New York: Knopf, 1996.

Sandler, Martin W. *Civil War*. New York: HarperCollins Juvenile Books, 1996.

Wisler, G. Clifton. *Mr. Lincoln's Drummer*. New York: Lodestar, 1995.

CD-ROM

American Heritage. *The Civil War: The Complete Multimedia Experience*. Simon & Schuster Interactive, 1995.

INTERNET RESOURCES

Library of Congress Civil War Photographs (1,118 photographs)
HTTP://RS6.LOC.GOV/CWPHOME.HTML

National Archives Photographs of the Civil War
HTTP://WWW.NARA.GOV

National Park Service Links to the Past
HTTP://CR.NPS.GOV

The United States Civil War Center, Louisiana State University.
HTTP://WWW.CWC.LSU.EDU

Index

Page numbers in *italics* refer to illustrations.